REVOLUTION
IN THE AGE OF
SOCIAL MEDIA

REVOLUTION IN THE AGE OF SOCIAL MEDIA

The Egyptian Popular Insurrection and the Internet

Linda Herrera

VERSO
London • New York

First published by Verso 2014
© Linda Herrera 2014

1 3 5 7 9 10 8 6 4 2

Verso
UK: 6 Meard Street, London W1F 0EG
US: 20 Jay Street, Suite 1010, Brooklyn, NY 11201
www.versobooks.com

Verso is the imprint of New Left Books

ISBN-13: 978-1-78168-275-3 (PBK)
ISBN-13: 978-1-78168-276-0 (HBK)
eISBN-13: 978-1-78168-277-7 (US)
eISBN-13: 978-1-78168-647-8 (UK)

British Library Cataloguing in Publication Data
A catalogue record for this book is available from the British Library

Library of Congress Cataloging-in-Publication Data

Herrera, Linda.
 Revolution in the age of social media : the Egyptian
popular insurrection and the Internet / Linda Herrera.
    pages cm
  Includes bibliographical references and index.
 ISBN 978-1-78168-275-3 (paperback) — ISBN 978-
1-78168-276-0 (hardback) — ISBN 978-1-78168-277-
7 (ebook)
 1. Egypt—History—Protests, 2011- 2. Internet—
Political aspects—Egypt. 3. Youth—Political
activity—Egypt. 4. Internet and youth—Political
aspects—Egypt. 5. Internet and activism—Egypt. I.
Title.
 DT107.87.H47 2014
 962.05'5—dc23
                                2014000584

Typeset in Minion Pro by MJ & N Gavan, Truro, Cornwall
Printed in the US by Maple Press

To the creative and courageous youth of Egypt who are engaged in an epic struggle to liberate their minds on the way to reimagining a new system for Egypt and the world

For last year's words belong to last year's language
And next year's words await another voice.
... What we call the beginning is often the end
And to make an end is to make a beginning.

"Little Gidding," T.S. Eliot

Contents

Acknowledgements

This book began as a "fast book" that turned into in a three-year odyssey. I first want to thank Ahmed Gaballah, a former student and research assistant from the American University in Cairo. He moved to California to work for Google where he helped develop the company's presence in the Middle East. He is now Senior Product Manager for Strategic Growth Markets at Adobe Systems. He introduced me to the inner workings of the Arabic web and walked me through techniques of online marketing. Together we read and reviewed the full 1,400-page printout of the "We Are All Khaled Said" Arabic Facebook page and worked together on Chapter 3, "Marketing Martyrdom." I am truly grateful for his energy in getting this project off the ground and for his sense of adventure.

I met Mark Lotfy, a filmmaker and virtual creator, during a visit to Egypt in the early phases of researching this book. We shared a common interest in understanding the power struggles taking place in virtual spaces. Mark's knowledge of the online culture wars, media theory, video games, and Egyptian popular culture is as astute and deep as anyone's. We coauthored an article for *Jadaliyya* called "E-Militias of the Muslim Brotherhood," and continued our collaboration by jointly writing chapters 6 and 7. He has read and commented on many parts of this book.

I have spent countless hours online and in Egypt with activists, students, artists, and friends old and new, all of whom are always incredibly generous with their time and insights. I extend a special thanks to AbdelRahman, Kholoud, Haitham, Aly, Dalia, Nur, Hossam, Nourhan, Sherif, Ahmed, and the many Facebook friends who always keep me abreast of ever-changing developments in Egypt.

Some of the ideas for this book took early form as *Jadaliyya* articles. I extend a big thanks to the tireless coeditors at *Jadaliyya*, Adel Iskandar, Toni Alessandri, Hesham Sallam, and Ziad Abu-Rish, for their feedback and comments on various articles. Thanks also to Peter Mandaville, who offered valuable comments on an earlier version of Chapter 3.

I began my position at the University of Illinois at Urbana-Champaign just nine days before the start of the January 25 Revolution. I have since shuttled between Illinois and Egypt on a regular basis. I am grateful for the tremendous support I have received from the university. Special thanks goes to colleagues at the College of Education at Illinois and specifically at the college's Department of Education Policy, Organization and Leadership, as well as to the Center for South Asia and Middle East Studies, and to my talented and eminently reliable teaching assistants, Fauzia Rahman, Garett Gietzen, Kevin Gitonga, and Ghassan Ibrahim, who have helped to keep me and my courses on track. Shiva, Tara, and Asef know how much I cherish their presence in my life.

CHAPTER ONE

Wired Youth Rise

In his memoir, *Revolution 2.0: The Power of the People Is Greater than the People in Power*, Wael Ghonim makes a startling revelation about his interrogation at the hands of Egyptian State Security during the January 25 Revolution. Ghonim was an anonymous administrator (admin) of the Arabic "We Are All Khaled Said" Facebook page that issued the call for revolution. He figured it was only a matter of time before he would be discovered. When two State Security agents captured him on January 27, 2011, outside a trendy Cairo restaurant, Ghonim assumed it was because of his work on the page. To his surprise, the interrogators had no idea he was working as an admin. They were solely interested in his ties to his American dinner companions. Ghonim, Google's head of marketing for the Middle East, had been in a meeting with Jared Cohen, director of Google Ideas and formerly of the United States Department of State, and Matthew Stepka, Google's VP for Strategy. These were the last people Ghonim saw before disappearing for eleven days. He writes, "Little did I know that this brief meeting would lead me to the most difficult experience of my life." On that same evening, Jared Cohen tweeted—rather indiscreetly given the risks faced by activists on the ground at the time—"For reliable on the ground resources in #Egypt (#jan25) follow @Ghonim @EgyptUpdates @alshaheeed." Alshaheeed, "The Martyr," was the Twitter handle for the "We Are All Khaled Said" page.

Ghonim recounts being blindfolded and taken away to an undisclosed location. During the interrogation, he was horrified to realize his questioners were trying to link him to the CIA. They were especially concerned about his relationship to Jared Cohen. Ghonim tries to downplay the State Security interest in Cohen by writing, "I didn't find it strange that they specifically asked about Jared. His Jewish-sounding name could raise eyebrows in Egyptian State Security, given the long-standing Arab-Israeli conflict." Ghonim's attempt to brush off questions about Cohen as mere sensitivity to a name is disingenuous at best. Cohen had held key positions in the State Department's internal think tank, Policy Planning, under both the Bush and Obama administrations. He had been pursuing a policy that can be called cyberdissident diplomacy (CDD) by reaching out to tech-savvy youth in the sixteen-to-thirty-five age range with the aim of training them in particular forms of cyberdissidence and online campaigning. Cohen's forte was building networks among young Muslims in the Middle East and North Africa (MENA) region. In 2010 he left the State Department to direct Google Ideas, where he specializes in finding technological approaches to "counterterrorism" and "counterradicalism."

The compelling story behind the youth-led revolt of 2011 is not quite the romantic tale of liberation through the emancipatory power of communications technologies that many had initially supposed it to be. Nor can Egypt's internet politics be reduced to widely circulating conspiracies about hidden hands from the United States and elsewhere orchestrating people and events from behind the scenes. But let us be clear: there are some hidden hands that do need to be brought to light and understood.

The uprising that began on January 25, 2011, and that continues in different forms to the present has been expressed in virtual spaces and on the streets. It is part of an ongoing youth-driven social upheaval born out of a technological revolution, a period of enhanced economic liberalization, the spread of international civil society initiatives, an escalation of military aggression in the region, and a tightening of the security state.

For the reader ready to balk at the proposition that the revolutionary movement has primarily been a youth movement, let us be clear. There is no doubt that the uprising that began on January 25, 2011, and that will undoubtedly reverberate far into the future has taken place on multiple fronts and involves vast segments of society. People from a wide cross section of the Egyptian populace harbor ample grievances against a system of power that is dehumanizing and supports rule by repressive autocrats. The people who participated in mass mobilizations against the Mubarak regime in 2011, the Supreme Council of Armed Forces (SCAF) in 2012, and the Muslim Brotherhood in 2013, have hailed from all generations and encompassed groups with diverse affiliations and social positions. The growing politicized classes include intersections of workers, students, women, children, the unemployed, white collar professionals, farmers, Islamists, Christians, atheists, liberals, artists—the list goes on. Our concern here is particularly with the growing and demographically dominant population of high school and university-educated youth born in the period from the 1970s to the early years of the millennium, who have been active in both virtual spaces and on the streets.

Prior to the Tunisian and Egyptian uprisings, the under-thirty-fives, who make up to 75 percent of the population in the MENA region, were mainly portrayed in policy, government, and academic circles as a "passive generation," or a generation "on hold." Yet it is this very generation that has been at the forefront of a cultural, intellectual, and political revolution that has been chipping away at the inevitability of the Old Order. Youth contain all the social, political, and economic variation that exists in society. Yet at the same time, members of this generation, particularly the wired among them, exhibit distinguishing features common to growing up in the virtual age. For instance, they display more fluid notions about privacy and value horizontal learning and sharing. They seem to consider it normal and acceptable to speak back to power, to interact across lines of difference, and to cultivate fictitious and anonymous public personas. As a collectivity, this generation has also shown itself to be assertive and ungovernable, characteristics that have developed as larger proportions of them have participated in the growing opposition culture, both online and offline. How did youth cultures begin transforming in the years leading up to the January 25 Revolution, and what does the politics of technology have to do with the changes?

The Awakening

In Egypt, the sleeper hit of the summer of 2006 was *Leisure Time* (*Awqat Faragh*), a film acclaimed for its realistic, gritty, and non-preachy depiction of Egyptian youth culture. The film captures the unmistakable crisis of being a young Arab. In the opening scene, three guys in their early twenties wander around aimlessly and ask each other, "What is there to do?" They feel misunderstood by their families, mistreated at work, uninterested in the university, and dissatisfied with love. To try to escape their boredom they dabble in drugs, pornography, sex, and Islamic piety, though nothing really helps. The purposelessness of their world leads one friend on a reckless path of death. At the end of the film, still at a loss as to how to get a handle on their lives, the three friends meet in an amusement park. They decide to take a ride on a cage-style Ferris wheel. The ride malfunctions when they are at the top of the wheel, rocking in midair. They cry out for help but no one hears. The closing shot of the film shows the three young men suspended in a cage and swaying in the wind. The image is powerful and the message clear: they are a suspended generation, in limbo, helpless, waiting to be rescued.

Fast forward to 2011. On January 14, 2011, the Arabic Facebook fan page titled "We Are All Khaled Said" (*Kulina Khaled Said*) was on fire. The page, which began in June 2010 in honor of its namesake, a young man from Alexandria allegedly killed at the hands of plainclothes police, blossomed into Egypt's most active and consequential anti-torture-campaign-turned-youth-movement in over half a century. This social media phenomenon crystallized a new kind of politics that was supposedly leaderless, horizontal, and networked, and that operated on a principle of online to offline mobilization. By January 2011, the page had grown to 390,000 members, 70 percent of whom were under twenty-four years old, and over 40 percent of whom were young women. It received a staggering nine million hits a day. In the wake of Tunisia's revolution, the "We Are All Khaled Said" Facebook page issued a call for an event, the "January 25 Revolution," which was to be Egypt's own revolution. The page did not cause the revolution, and youth of the internet (*shabab al-internet*) were not the only group active in it, but it is hard to imagine the revolt being put into motion without, firstly, the Tunisian revolution, and, secondly, the changing political culture, mentality, and networked behavior of Egypt's wired youth.

When the world learned that Egypt's revolution was supposedly triggered by a Facebook page, a clamor erupted between the internet utopians and internet skeptics, between the proponents of the "new" politics of globalized networked multitudes as theorized by the likes of Manuel Castells, Michael Hardt, and Antonio Negri, and the "old" politics of traditional movement building. Figures from the left of the political spectrum balked at the suggestion that "Facebook youth" should be taken seriously, or that US tech companies like Facebook, Twitter, and Google, which embody the capitalist ideals of free market America, could be factors in an actual revolution, or in any movement that challenges the dominant global system. In his book *The Rebirth of History: Times of Riots and Uprisings*, French philosopher Alain Badiou cuttingly writes: "Some commentators have regarded the role of 'youth' in the riots in the Arab world as a sociological novelty, and have linked it to the use of Facebook or other vacuities of alleged technical innovation in the postmodern age. But who has ever seen a riot whose front ranks were made up of the elderly?" In his cavalier dismissal of youth and social media, Badiou exhibits a deep misunderstanding of the radical transformation that has been occurring in Arab societies—a transformation that extends far beyond the traditional political sphere and that has featured wired youth at the forefront.

This generation has experienced exponential rates of connectivity while suffering from systematic disenfranchisement, especially when it comes to institutions of the state and the economy. Young people have had to contend with the dismantling of social safety nets, record high rates of youth unemployment, and spiking rates of inequality. If older cohorts who came of age between the 1950s and 1980s viewed the state as a repressive yet benevolent behemoth—since it provided affordable housing, education, government jobs, and food subsidies—the current generation experiences the state as purely rapacious, authoritarian, and indifferent. A twenty-five-year-old Egyptian university graduate illustrates this difference when he says, "I mainly associate the state with the horrible experience of having to go the police station to get my [national] ID." To better understand how this wired generation started to coalesce into a counter-power requires going back to the era of technological opening. The high-tech revolution arrived in Egypt with a combination of excitement, moral panic, and desire. No one could predict how technology would change people and society, or how people would alter the technology.

Liberalization Egyptian Style

The Egyptian government, historically reluctant to allow the spread of technologies that would loosen its grip on its citizenry, nevertheless opened its doors to information and communication technologies (ICT) and the liberalization of the media. The transition to an "information society," otherwise called a "knowledge economy," came about through a combination of pressure and opportunity. The countries of the Organisation for Economic Cooperation and Development (OECD), the United Nations, the World Bank, and the International Monetary Fund (IMF) tied any number of loans and trade agreements to Egypt's willingness to sync its national economy with the knowledge economy in which OECD countries held a clear advantage. At the same time, an ICT-driven economy would allow Egypt to more fully participate in the global marketplace, with its promise of profits and economic growth.

As video games, satellite dishes, mobile phones, and the internet became more important to Egyptian society, these technologies did indeed bring a vigorous boost to the economy. They also contributed to a breakdown of traditional authority and control. The state tried its best to curb the "negative effects" of technology. The bureaucratic fixes proved especially ineffective when it came to controlling the "deviant" behavior of the new generation of tech-consuming kids. As the young absorbed the new technologies into their lives, starting early on with video games, these technologies made cracks in the traditional authority system of the family, state, and religious institutions.

The children's game market entered the Arab region in the 1980s with the Japanese brand Sakhr, coproduced with the Kuwaiti company Al-Alamiah. It was one of the most successful products in the Arab world until production abruptly ceased after Iraq invaded Kuwait in 1990, a reminder of the correlation between geopolitics, security, and business. A children's video culture quickly developed around the imported games, whose characters and recreated environments were exogenous to the Arab world. Children would gather in the homes of middle- and high-class families, where they would play the games for hours, amazed by the magic of this new virtual space. Regardless of whether they won or lost, the players played the games endlessly, since they could be reincarnated ad infinitum, game after game. In the 1990s, Sakhr was replaced by

Game Boy, which was later overtaken by PlayStation. Children who grew up with video games developed a taste for being masters of story and character, and they got accustomed to a high degree of interactivity. The video game market was a booming business, with profits surpassing those of even the famed Egyptian cinema.

Video games first took off in the homes of affluent families, but soon entered arcades and cybercafes, where they were available for rent. A social worker in Cairo recounted that even street children, through stealing and begging, cobbled together enough money to enjoy the thrill of playing video games for an hour or two. She observed that whereas they once used stolen money to buy drugs, they now used the money to play video games. This phenomenon of playing games with stolen money occurred not only among the poorest children, but also among youth from more affluent families. In middle- and high-class homes where parents placed restrictions on their children's game-playing, their children sometimes stole money to feed their gaming addictions. The video game generation would rise up during the revolution and carry some practices it learned from the world of games into the streets.

The Egyptian state did not seem alarmed about the growing video game market. It was far more concerned about the growth of independent media and communications technologies, which infringed directly on the state's traditional jurisdiction. The satellite dish—known as "*el-dish*" or "*el-Taba3*"—is a case in point. *El-dish* arrived in 1992 as a high-end, luxury commodity, costing roughly from $5,000 to $10,000. Its penetration was limited to international five-star hotel chains and expensive lounges and cafes. At that time, Egyptians could choose among a handful of state-controlled television channels.

In 1998 the first mass-market satellite dish was introduced into the Egyptian market, an Israeli brand called The Benjamin. At a purchase price of around $1,000, the cost was high relative to household income, but the dish was within reach of the middle classes thanks to popular installment plans and cost-sharing arrangements. Neighbors in apartment buildings pooled their resources to buy a single dish and split the connection across apartments. The entrance of Chinese dishes into the market around 2005 pushed prices down even further.

In Egypt, anywhere from 20 to 43 percent of the population lives below the poverty line, but that did not stop broad swaths of the population from finding creative, innovative, and at times illegal ways to get their hands on the dish and every subsequent new technology. In lower-income neighborhoods and informal communities, there was a parallel market for used and refurbished satellite dishes. A used dish could be bought for less than half the price of The Benjamin. Neighbors divided the cost and connected the dish across not only multiple apartments in a building, but between adjacent buildings. For the more cash-strapped consumer, wannabe hackers came up with an even more economical workaround, The Satellite Thief (*Harami al-Dish*). This makeshift signal-hopper was made out of a mix of stolen pieces of satellite dishes, cooking pots, wire fragments, mirror shards, aluminum foil, and duct tape, all for a price of less than ten dollars. In their turn, cell phones, video games, and computers would follow similar patterns of entering the market at high prices, but then falling within reach of large sectors of the population in a relatively short period.

With the spread of *el-dish*, ordinary Egyptians could peruse a wide range of programs. Satellite television, like the internet after it, was initially known as a source for entertainment and pornography, but it was not long before Egyptians developed a voracious appetite for news, religious programming, and Arabic talk shows. With the launch of Al Jazeera (1996), followed by Al Arabiya (2003), and BBC Arabic (2008), news became an essential staple in the Arab media diet.

Arabic satellite programming was taking off just as the US was in the early stages of spectacularly unpopular wars in Iraq and Afghanistan. These wars provided ample fodder for the Arabic satellite news networks, whose coverage fueled already strong anti-American sentiments in the region. The US government sought to turn Arab public opinion in its favor by operating its own Arabic satellite news channel, similar to what it has long done through its federal funded radio station Voice of America (VOA). In 2004, the US Congress funded a twenty-four-hour Arabic news channel, Alhurra, to the tune of $90 million. The channel was launched on Feb 14, 2004 and transmitted to twenty-two Arab countries. Weary of the American bias of Alhurra and not wanting for choice, Arabic viewers rejected the late-to-market channel. It fell flat. The US government sought to influence public opinion through new media technologies, but the experiment with Alhurra proved that satellite television was not going to be the outlet to do so.

If the satellite dish opened Egyptian society to alternative viewpoints, the mobile phone gave individuals the freedom of unmediated communication and the ability to spread messages across vast mobile networks. Anyone with a mobile phone could talk and communicate away from the home or office, where colleagues and families monitored their communication.

In 1990 an Egyptian household had to wait between one and eight years to obtain a government-controlled landline. At any point the government could wiretap a phone, intercept communications, or cut off a line altogether. In 1997 Egyptian business mogul Nagib Saweris founded Mobinil, the first mobile communications company in Egypt. A year later, Vodafone came onto the market and price competition began. At the beginning of the millennium, mobile phones were considered a luxury product. By 2007, with the founding of the third company, Etisalat Misr, phones became a basic necessity for Egyptians across all layers of society. Not owning a mobile phone became tantamount to not having shoes. With over 56.5 million phones in circulation in 2010 (a 72 percent penetration rate), the vast majority of Egyptians carried a mobile phone.

Phone networks, in addition to facilitating conventional

communication, enabled a new kind of social theater. Resourceful and imaginative Egyptians saw in the mushrooming phone networks an opportunity to create free radio stations. Creators anonymously crafted original comic skits and stories which people circulated from phone to phone as recorded voice messages. Some of the early skits that went viral ridiculed the excessive piety of religious figures. In 2008, for instance, an especially popular comedy sketch poked fun at a Muslim sheikh who was so pious that even during a mundane conversation on a bus he spoke in the lofty and antiquated style of Quranic recitation. In another episode, a character impersonating a priest chanted in the style of Coptic monks to tell the story of a fictitious saint with the comical name Avatatas. He related in hilarious detail how Saint Avatatas was in a car accident and, since he considered all dimensions of his life as holy, told people to cover themselves with the sacred oil of his smashed car. Saint Avatatas, who came to life on cellphone networks, became one of the only Coptic comic characters to enter Egyptian popular culture. Over time, mass phone messages became more overtly political, especially in the lead-up to parliamentary elections in 2010, where phone networks were used for spreading campaign news and rumors alike about the candidates.

Even as the Egyptian government committed itself to liberalizing communications and media, it did so with a high degree of trepidation. The regime continued to be essentially authoritarian and the heavy-handed presence of the police state remained intact. As technologies became more advanced, the government continued to try to censor media content and monitor citizens' communications. Slavoj Žižek refers to economic liberalization without political liberalization as "authoritarian capitalism," or "capitalism with Asian values."

The government ministries that oversaw the communications and information sectors enforced rules on service providers so that they could track citizens and link phone numbers, and later IP addresses, to individuals and households. This tracking system provided some assurances to the government, but it couldn't keep up with either the pace of technological change or people's own ingenuity. In actuality, when Egypt opened its doors to private high-tech media and communications companies in the 1990s, its system of control, surveillance, and censorship quickly began to collapse. As satellite dishes, mobile phones, video games, computers, and internet service providers flooded the country, people gained a window onto the world and an ability to interact with it in ways unimaginable just a few years before.

Cultural Spring

Internet use in Egypt, a country of some 83 million people, has spread at a staggering rate, especially among fifteen- to thirty-five-year-olds. In the year 2000 there were a mere 300,000 users, a number that increased to six million by 2006, 10.5 million in 2008, and over seventeen million in 2010. In 2009, Egypt was estimated to have anywhere from 35,000 to 160,000 bloggers. Technology remains unevenly distributed, but even in contexts where many young people do not have access to digital media, the few who do have access drive generational change with far-reaching cultural and political consequences.

Scores of people in the region have used the internet in ways that open cultural frontiers, improve language and artistic abilities, break boundaries, and shatter taboos. In 2004, young Egyptians used the internet for many activities including chatting, consulting religious opinions, setting up study groups, exchanging photos, watching porn, playing games, following sports, listening to music, spreading jokes, and flirting. One activity that especially stood out was their construction of an alternative news universe online. Young users who may not have been inclined towards politics started to take part in a budding youth culture where it was trendy to express opinions about the government and current events.

The new communication technologies also allowed people to

flout societal norms around segregation. As they communicated directly via phone networks and congregated in virtual spaces, people mixed and mingled in ways that were difficult in the physical world. The effects were most immediately noticeable among young Egyptian women. When a young woman used her mobile phone or went online, she experienced a form of autonomy that was lacking in the family and at school, where social control was pervasive and adults constantly monitored her behavior.

Take the case of twenty-two-year-old Mona, who grew up in a culturally conservative and religiously pious home. In 2004, when she was in high school, her parents bought a computer on installment. Mona was curious about other cultures and started visiting chat rooms to practice her English and meet foreigners. The platform of choice in Egypt at that time was ICQ, an instant messaging program owned by the Israeli company Mirabilis and later sold to America Online (AOL).

At first, Mona was reluctant to chat with boys online, since in her everyday life she rarely spoke with boys who weren't part of her family. But when she was in a chat room and met a boy from New Zealand who was looking for answers about Islam, she convinced herself there could not possibly be any harm in talking about religion. The two of them developed an online friendship. That experience served as a gateway to more daring behavior. She later sought out and chatted with other "taboo" groups and broached more controversial subjects. She reached out to Israelis because, as she explained, "We hear a lot about them in the news, and I wanted to know them firsthand. It was normal. There was no big problem."

Emboldened by the freedom of movement and expression they experienced in chat rooms, young women soon took to blogging in large numbers. Fatin, an undergraduate student at Alexandria University who majored in psychology, talked about the great pleasure she experienced when she started blogging with a group of friends in 2005: "I felt I wanted to open up, and I loved writing.

Also, I wanted to see my words online … I just loved it." Her group consisted of both boys and girls from her university. They blogged anonymously about their private lives and politics, and they pushed boundaries as they explored taboo subjects such as relationships between the sexes, religious discrimination, and doubts about God.

Bloggers, most of whom were initially anonymous, came to know each other's personas online and built networks and virtual communities. In 2006, for instance, a group of Egyptian bloggers who wrote about women's issues joined forces to launch a website and campaign called "We Are All Laila" (*Kulina Laila*). The initiative was spearheaded by a blogger who went by the pseudonym Lasto Adri (I Don't Know). She reached out to several Arab women bloggers and proposed that they come together one day a year under the banner "We Are All Laila" to blog about problems and challenges facing Arab women. The name "Laila" was inspired by the main character of the novel *The Open Door* by the Egyptian novelist Latifa El Zayyat. "Open door" refers to the first wave of Egypt's economic liberalization that took place under the presidency of Anwar Sadat (1970–1981). As explained in English on the "We Are All Laila" website:

> Laila represents every Egyptian girl who suffers oppression and injustice in the Egyptian Eastern society during the time of the Suez Canal Crisis, when Egypt was attacked by Israel, The United Kingdom and France. The novel also features Laila's struggle with the community to prove the importance of the role of women in this society. The organizers confirm that the oppression Laila goes through, throughout the novel, is not so different from the current status of women in Arab societies today.

Young women multiplied online, where they raised their voices and boldly asserted their presence. They stirred the ire of conservative and paternalistic forces in society, who subscribed to the view that women should comport themselves with modesty and restraint, including in virtual spaces. The leadership of the Muslim Brotherhood condemned in especially harsh terms the presence of young women in the blogosphere. In 2006, the following question appeared on the Muslim Brotherhood website: "Would you marry a girl who blogs?" Certain sheikhs had already weighed in on this question by issuing fatwas arguing that young women's participation in online discussions, chat rooms, and blogs constituted punishable behavior.

The younger, tech-savvy members of the Brotherhood found these types of arguments preposterous and hopelessly out of date. Starting in about 2007, a critical mass from among the younger generation of the Muslim Brotherhood, many of whom were the children of professionals who worked for an extended period in Arab Gulf countries, started defecting from the group. For twenty-three-year-old Ahmed, the last straw was when Brotherhood elders reprimanded him for posting his photo online. At that time, the Brotherhood's online forums banned their members, male and female, from posting their pictures since this act could cause "chaos" (*fitna*). Ahmed recalls, "It was an amazing experience. They were acting like big extremists." In response to this absurd directive, he and his friend swapped their profile photos so they could claim they were posting not their own photo, but someone else's photo. The Brotherhood later relaxed its position on online photos.

In the Brotherhood, rifts along generational lines only became more accelerated over time. As the younger members experienced a degree of autonomy, freedom of expression, and diversity online, the Brotherhood maintained its rigid demand for obedience. "Somaya," a young woman from a well-known Muslim Brotherhood family, explained that many of the young people who left the group remained committed to the Brotherhood's Islamic orientation, but they could no longer abide by its top-down, non-democratic governing structure, or its outdated attitudes about communication and the internet. "It's not that we no longer carry the Brotherhood line of thought," she said. "Our aim is rather to apply our thought, our Muslim way of life, to other currents like liberalism, Marxism, and socialism. The point is that the older [members of the Brotherhood] don't see our experiences as valuable and don't really support us [or understand] the ways we are changing." Her friend Ahmed, also a former member of the Brotherhood, chimed in: "We are not liberals or socialists. We are just people reconsidering our identities and the basis for our ideas." Ahmed described his group of friends as having a "postmodern Islamic identity," meaning they were more flexible when it came to interacting with members of the opposite sex, people of different religions, and people from the other side of the political spectrum.

Somaya and Ahmed met through the online discussion forum "Army for Mental Freedom" (*Geish lil Tahrir al-Fikry*), which deals with how to liberate the mind from the education system. They also interacted regularly on a blog devoted to the question of why Egyptians emigrate. Like countless other Egyptians, they began an acquaintance online around a set of issues that translated to campaigning and political mobilization offline. Though they had been exchanging views for over three years online, it was not until the January 25 Revolution that they met in person for the first time, in Tahrir Square.

Politics After the Fall of Baghdad

For many young, internet-savvy Egyptians, the road to Tahrir very likely began with the fall of Baghdad. Baghdad is a living city in its own right, but as the seat of the Abbasid Dynasty during the Golden Age of Islam (750–1258), it is also a place of immense historical value and symbolic importance. I was living in Cairo at the time of the "Shock and Awe" bombardment of Baghdad by US forces. I witnessed ordinary Egyptians literally weeping in the streets as they watched the destruction of Baghdad on televisions in outdoor cafes. The fall and decimation of Baghdad was a turning point for Egyptians, especially for the nascent internet activists among them.

Prior to the war on Iraq, Egyptian cyberactivists had participated in networks around the cause of Palestine, especially from the time of the Second Intifada, which started in 2000. Cyberactivists joined solidarity campaigns and boycotts, and coordinated local demonstrations in support of Palestinians in the West Bank and Gaza. Those activist efforts, though important, did not begin to approximate the massive online mobilization that helped form a global anti-war movement against the planned US-led invasion of Iraq in 2003. Through online networks, anti-war protesters in Europe, the US, Egypt, and around the globe coordinated a day of street demonstrations on February 15, 2003. People in over six hundred cities took part in what turned out to be the largest coordinated activist event to date. On February 17, 2003, Patrick Tyler wrote in an op-ed for the *New York Times*:

> The fracturing of the Western alliance over Iraq and the huge antiwar demonstrations around the world this weekend are reminders that there may still be two superpowers on the planet: the United States and world public opinion ... An exceptional phenomenon has appeared on the streets of world cities.

Despite the massive outpouring of dissent worldwide, the war on Iraq went forward. It stirred deep feelings of injustice and anger across the globe, but perhaps most acutely in the Arab world.

In 2003, three Egyptians living in London—two brothers and a cousin in their thirties—felt impotent as they watched the bombardment of Baghdad. They wanted to do something about it. They came up with the idea of starting a virtual platform that would bring about real change in Egypt. In 2004 they launched a website called "The Change" (*Al Taghrir*).[1] In an interview with the author in June 2012, one of the founders, Wael Adel, explained:

It was the fall of Baghdad in 2003 that made us feel like there was no hope. We realized that all these political movements on the ground weren't making any difference. We knew that we needed to change the mentality of Egyptians, to bring about a *mindquake*, an earthquake in the mind, to arm Egyptians with action tools. We, the people, have all the power. But we couldn't figure out how to put our power to work in the right direction. When people have ideas they can make change happen. We focused on changing the way people think. The mentality of the people.

They hunted for good ideas in online forums and looked to other countries and histories for inspiration. They were especially inspired by the experiences coming from the Iranian Revolution, Sudanese politics, the Eastern European revolutions, and the Allende period in Chile. The group claims complete independence, but acknowledges being influenced by the Qatari professor Yasim Sultan, one of the founders of the Muslim Brotherhood in Qatar, who lived in Egypt for seven years and had a deep understanding of the Egyptian political situation. When he was twenty-six, Wael Adel studied with Sultan.

The Change was a daring website for the time. It depicted Hosni Mubarak in the guise of a pharaoh, a caricature that would eventually become commonplace, but that had shock value at first. Since the website was housed on a British server, it was outside the jurisdiction and censorship of Egyptian authorities. The group tested ideas and experimented with ways to attract young Egyptians to politics in fun and entertaining ways. The website hosted music for download and served as a portal for movies about political movements in countries like Serbia and Chile.

The Change evolved into a larger platform and training unit for cyberactivists, rebranding itself as "The Academy of Change." The founders registered it as a legal organization in London (2006), Qatar (2009), and Austria (2010). The Academy website was a gateway to a wealth of free resources in Arabic and English about how to plan nonviolent civil disobedience campaigns and protests. After the January 25 event, it was revealed that the Academy was involved in training and networking with key activists involved in online campaigns and movements, including from the "We Are All Khaled Said" page.

From roughly 2004, cyberactivism became a staple of the Egyptian political landscape. Political groups, campaigns, and social movements recognized the importance of establishing a presence online. Opposition parties, from the Muslim Brotherhood to the Communist Party, launched their own websites and blogs that were run by their younger technologically adept members. One movement in particular—The Kefaya movement (est. 2004), officially named "The Egyptian Movement for Change"—adapted the principle of horizontal organizing and networking from online activism to its on-the-ground presence. The organizational structure of Kefaya was starkly different from the stodgy party politics that had dominated the Egyptian opposition for decades. The group brought together a coalition of leftists, Islamists, and Nasserists, who united to challenge the legitimacy of Mubarak's rule, call for the end to the Emergency Law, and advocate for constitutional reform and genuine representative democracy. This coalition crossed lines of generation, religion, gender, and ideology. A young Kefaya member and blogger, Wael Abbas, set up the website "Egyptian Awareness" to report on Kefaya activities.

When Kefaya held an anti-Mubarak demonstration, the wired members among them splashed the event all over the internet, thereby amplifying its effect and building support and solidarity both inside and outside the country. They spread their messages through blogs and online forums and put into circulation the group's chants that were daring for the time, such as "Down, down, with Hosni Mubarak!" (*yaskut yaskut Hosni Mubarak*). Armed with cell phones and other recording devices, members took photos and videos of their demonstrations and recorded the disproportionate use of police against them. The images circulated online and were sometimes picked up by the international press and caused the regime grave public relations embarrassments. Even after the group disbanded, Kefaya remained a critical reference point for horizontal coalition politics.

Egypt's parliamentary and first multi-candidate presidential elections in 2005 served as crucial milestones in the evolution of online opposition politics. Young citizens took it upon themselves to document and publicize the array of fraud and intimidation against candidates and voters. Haitham, a blogger who was nineteen years old at the time, took his first steps toward citizen journalism in 2005. He explains:

> I was very interested in carrying out an experiment to supervise an election from inside a poll station. I went to a small village outside of Alexandria and started to monitor what was happening. I saw how people would sell their votes and write "yes" for Mubarak just for money. I took pictures and posted them on my blog.

He wasn't working for a particular political party or candidate, just acting as an independent citizen with an online voice. Throughout Egypt—in Aswan, Mansoura, and Cairo—other bloggers, some as young as fifteen and sixteen years old, carried out similar experiments.

The blogosphere in 2005 was especially ablaze with the scandal of the arrest of the forty-one-year-old presidential candidate and parliamentarian Ayman Nour. This rising politician and chairman of the Al-Ghad Party (Tomorrow Party) attracted large numbers of young urban supporters. In January 2005, Nour was charged with forging documents connected to the formation of his party. Nevertheless, he still won 7 percent of the vote (according to the official tally), coming in second behind Mubarak. He was imprisoned from 2005 to 2009, but consistently pleaded innocence. US Secretary of State Condoleezza Rice personally intervened to pressure the Mubarak government to release Nour and uphold its promises of electoral reform, but with little success. The flurry of pressure and activity online and offline did not save Nour from prison or alter the results of these highly fraudulent elections. However, the 2005 election cycle emboldened the opposition and scores of ordinary citizens, who took matters into their own hands with their blogs, recording devices, and coalition groups.

From roughly 2006, on the heels of the elections and with the availability of YouTube, online political agitation took another turn. A critical mass of activists took up human rights and anti-torture blogging. YouTube provided activists with the opportunity to post videos of police violence, in a tactic of naming and shaming. Wael Abbas, who had started the Kefaya website and later became known as an anti-torture watchdog, gained notoriety in human rights circles after he posted a video clip of two police officers torturing and sodomizing a minibus driver, Emad El Kabir, with a rod. Not only did the horrifying and graphic video go viral, but, at the urging of human rights activists, El Kabir came forward and pressed charges against his torturers. In an unprecedented victory, the police officers involved in the crime were each sentenced to five years in prison. Following the incident, the Egyptian authorities forbade mobile phones in police stations.

By 2007–2008, blogging was being surpassed by other forms of social media. The end of blogging and the rise of Facebook involved some gains but also came with certain losses. Bloggers generally put great care into the craft of writing and the aesthetics of their blogs. They developed a unique voice and audience, and in the process they built their personalities and even developed leadership attributes. With the rise of social media, the voices of many celebrated bloggers faded.

In contrast to blogs, social media rewards networking, speed, brevity, and creativity. The virtual architecture of social media also happens to be especially well suited for politics oriented towards single-issue campaigns. In 2008, a new chapter in political organizing—this time using social media—transformed Egypt's political scene. In March 2008, Israa Abdel Fatah, a one-time member of the youth wing of the Al-Ghad Party, received a text message from twenty-eight-year-old Ahmed Maher, an engineering student and activist. As reported in a *New York Times* article entitled "Revolution, Facebook-Style," he suggested that the two of them arrange a general strike to support a strike planned for April 6 by textile workers in the Nile Delta city of Al Mahalla al-Kubra. Israa had set up Facebook events before, such as for a film about torture that attracted one hundred or so of her Facebook friends. She duly set up the April 6 event, expecting it to attract the same circle of friends. Instead, it unexpectedly went viral. As described in the *New York Times* article: "Almost as soon as she set up the group, there were 16 members; when she refreshed the page a few minutes later, there were more than 60. The next day, more than 1,000. [Israa] watched with fear and excitement as thousands of people, then tens of thousands, started joining and posting to the group. Eventually, the number reached 76,000. As the group's administrators, she and Maher … took turns monitoring the site day and night."

In this way, the Facebook group called the "6th of April Youth Movement" (*Harakat Shabab 6 Abril*) was born. For all the advantages of Facebook organizing, it also carries heavy risks. The two creators of the 6th of April event were arrested and jailed. In one confrontation with State Security police, Maher was beaten for twelve hours in an effort to make him disclose his Facebook password, which he never did. His friend Wael Abbas posted images of Maher's bruised and beaten body on his blog.

Many people who attended the on-the-ground protest in Al Mahalla al-Kubra used the recently available micro-blogging tool Twitter to coordinate their movements and share information about the whereabouts of police. Biz Stone, Twitter cofounder, expressed his amazement at how Egyptians used Twitter in ways its inventors could not have imagined. In an interview with Terri Gross on *Fresh Air* he said,

When we heard … that Twitter was being used in Egypt in 2008 to organize these protests, that was one of the early, eye-opening experiences for us, that made us realize this was not just something in the Bay Area for, you know, technical geeks to fool around with and to find out what each other's up to, but a global communications system that could be used for almost anything and everything.

The corporate media and blogosphere, including the *New York Times* and *Wired*, picked up on the story of Egypt's 6th of April strike. The terms "Facebook revolution" and "Twitter revolution" were used in relation to Egypt and later applied to Moldova, Iran, and Tunisia in 2009, 2010, and 2011 respectively. As Egypt's young citizens were being touted on the world stage for using the tools of the information age for freedom struggles, there was an underlying message that their freedom, as inspiring as it was, needed to be contained and directed. For if left to their own devices, there was no telling how Egypt's dynamic youth of the internet might use their newfound power.

In Walks the State Department

In November 2008, with only two months remaining in President George W. Bush's second term, the US State Department launched a new initiative, the Alliance of Youth Movements (AYM). Standing at the podium to give the press briefing were James K. Glassman, Under Secretary of State for Public Diplomacy, and Jared Cohen, from the staff of Policy Planning. Conceptualized as an initiative to fight youth extremism and violence, AYM fit squarely in the post-9/11 "War on Terror" era.

Glassman made special reference to Egypt's 6th of April Youth Movement, which would be represented at the forthcoming AYM summit:

Let me mention the Egypt group, which is among the best known of the groups that … will be there, the Shabab 6 of April, which has emerged as Egypt's largest pro-democracy youth group … [In] April, the group staged a countrywide protest that led to some crackdowns by the government that led to some arrests and even deaths. And some of the leaders were tortured, severely beaten, and an effort … that backfired somewhat when pictures of their injuries were posted online. There's actually a good piece about this group in … *WIRED*. And we will have some members from this group coming.

Glassman explained that through an AYM summit, the State Department would bring together top bloggers, cyberdissidents, the US government, and US corporations. In fact, AYM began as a partnership among the US Department of State, Howcast Media, Google, Facebook, MTV, PepsiCo, Causecast.org, and the advertising and marketing firm Omnicom Group, among other US corporations. Glassman acknowledged that the State Department's role was limited to that of facilitator or convener and said, "We really can't serve to actually build these groups ourselves. They would … not have very much in the way of credibility." Rather, the State Department's role was to work behind the scenes to help activists build networks and to facilitate the production and dissemination of cyberactivist training materials.

Why would the State Department want to empower young cybercitizens of Egypt and other Muslim-majority counties in the Middle East? Did the State Department think it would advance its post-9/11 democracy-promotion agenda in Egypt and the wider region, while also promoting American businesses in the region? The answers can be found in excavating a policy that we will call "cyberdissident diplomacy."

CHAPTER TWO

Cyberdissident Diplomacy

Place the young at the head of the insurgent masses; you do not know what strength is latent in those young bands, what magic influence the voices of the young have on the crowd; you will find in them a host of apostles for the new religion. But youth lives on movement, grows great in enthusiasm and faith. Consecrate them with a lofty mission; inflame them with emulation and praise; spread through their ranks the word of fire, the word of inspiration; speak to them of country, of glory, of power, of great memories.

The above quote from Italian nationalist Guiseppe Mazzini opens the 2003 report "The Youth Factor: The New Demographics of the Middle East and the Implications for U.S. Policy." The report, authored by Graham Fuller, formerly of the CIA, US Foreign Service, and RAND Corporation, joined a chorus of voices from the Washington, DC establishment in the post-9/11 and post-Cold War era trumpeting the need to contain and capture the hearts and minds of Arab and Muslim youth through "soft power." With up to 75 percent of the population of the Middle East and North Africa (MENA) region under thirty-five years old, the young were well placed to act as what Mazzini calls the "apostles for a new religion." And that new religion, as Fuller and numerous analysts of his ilk make clear, is a form of liberalism with a pro-American and pro–free market bent. Fuller writes: "Liberalization of Middle

Eastern societies is perhaps the single most urgent task in averting the negative effects of this demographic shift." He puts forward a familiar argument about the need for Arab and Muslim societies to liberalize in the image and under the supervision of the West, but he is short on specifics.

To arrive at a more cogent policy framework, then-Secretary of State Colin Powell formed a US government Advisory Group on Public Diplomacy in the Arab and Muslim World, headed by US diplomat Edward Djerejian. The keystone report of the "Djerejian Group," entitled "Changing Minds, Winning Peace: A New Strategic Direction for U.S. Public Diplomacy in the Arab & Muslim World" (2003), outlines a nine-part strategy with information and communication technologies (ICT) at its center. The report laments the US government's shortsightedness in divesting from media and information programs after the end of the Cold War, and calls on the government to substantially reinvest in these vital "weapons of advocacy." The report firmly asserts that ICT should become the top priority for public diplomacy, superseding even the long-standing educational exchange programs.

"Public diplomacy" refers to ways the US government promotes and protects its national security, economic, and political interests by reaching out to foreign publics, as distinct from working through formal diplomatic channels. Public diplomacy uses persuasion, or "soft power," to achieve its objectives, as opposed to force, or "hard power," which is the prerogative of the military and other coercive organs of the state. The guru of soft power, Joseph S. Nye Jr., reinforces the point that in the information age, the key to winning over Muslim youth is through reaching their minds. In his 2009 *Foreign Affairs* article "Get Smart" he writes:

> In today's information age, success is the result not merely of whose army wins but also of whose story wins. The current struggle against Islamist terrorism is much less a clash of civilizations than an ideological struggle within Islam. The United States cannot

win unless the Muslim mainstream wins ... Many Muslims disagree with American values as well as American policies, but that does not mean that they agree with bin Laden ... Soft power is needed to reduce the extremists' numbers and win the hearts and minds of the mainstream.

This line of reasoning presumes that the "Muslim mainstream" is not capable of finding its own path to moderation and democracy. It neither recognizes nor gives credence to those indigenous voices and social movements that reject the medley of violent extremism, dictatorship, and militarism. By its very nature, this approach to soft power precludes any genuine dialogue with independent local actors in the region and displays indifference to their positions and aspirations. Instead, public policy puts in place strategies with the aim of co-opting the voices of moderation.

Over the past decade, there has been an ongoing debate in Washington, DC about how to improve the tools of "ideological warfare" and overhaul the machinery of public diplomacy in the communications age. The Center for the Study of the Presidency and Congress has weighed in heavily on this debate. It advocates privatizing US public diplomacy and treating it as a "Marshall Plan for the hearts and minds of the world's youth," especially Arab and Muslim youth.

In the Center's 2003 report, "An Initiative: Strengthening US-Muslim Communications," Cold War diplomat Max Kampelman laments the diminished reputation of the US in the Arab world and calls on allies to help repair it. He writes:

Our reputation in the world, particularly among Arabs, has significantly declined. For shortsighted reasons, we disarmed ourselves of the weapons of ideological warfare ... We need new and additional resources. We need eloquent, effective pro-American and pro-democratic spokespeople and organized groups of champions. We must win the war of ideas.

The report does not suggest the obvious, namely that the US reputation in the region suffered a heavy blow because of its enormously unpopular, disruptive, and non-UN-sanctioned war in Iraq. Instead of offering advice along the lines of ending the war and starting a process of paying reparations, actions that would undoubtedly go far in rehabilitating the US's standing in the region, the experts search for ways to make the Arab public pro-US *despite* the war. They advocate for the need to influence youth public opinion by infiltrating their communications spaces and networks and spreading pro-US messages.

In 2003, as people in Egypt were innovatively using phone networks to circulate popular skits and political messages, the State Department followed their lead. In Cairo the public affairs section of the US embassy started circulating short messages about the US President and Secretary of State to a list of Egyptian cell phone numbers. Unlike the homegrown skits that went viral as people voluntarily passed them from phone to phone, the pro-US messages generally traveled unidirectionally from the embassy to the targeted phone. There were also attempts to penetrate the most popular online chat rooms of young Arabs, but this proved far more difficult due to the atomized and interactive nature of chat rooms. Chat rooms, like social media after it, do not lend themselves to packaged, top-down messaging in the style of traditional media, but rely on people-to-people crowdsourcing. Christopher Ross, Special Coordinator for Public Diplomacy at the State Department, describes the difficulty of working in chat rooms:

> There are many, many chat rooms in which the Middle East, and U.S. policy towards the Middle East, are openly discussed. Many of their participants are from the Middle East. We are not present. And the difficulty is that to be present is very labor-intensive. But it is an issue that we're looking at.

As the State Department's Policy Planning staff was formulating ideas about how to reach the wired youth in MENA countries by penetrating their communication spaces, the United States Agency for International Development (USAID) looked towards strengthening capacity in more traditional areas of civil society. It established the Middle East Partner Initiative (MEPI) in 2002 to "help democracy to spread, education to thrive, economies to grow, and women to be empowered." After its initial reliance on USAID, MEPI was taken over fairly quickly by the State Department's Near Eastern Affairs Bureau and initially run by Elizabeth Cheney, daughter of Vice President Dick Cheney, followed by Tamara Wittes and Nazanin Ash.

In its first two years, MEPI supported a number of standard democracy-promotion activities in line with Bush's "Freedom Agenda," such as voter education, youth leadership training, judicial reform, media monitoring, journalism skills workshops, and training in the newspaper business. In an interview with the Carnegie Endowment for International Peace in 2005 about the goals of MEPI, Cheney talked about the need to provide people in the MENA countries with access to media, and to give the "non-extremist" voice a platform:

> For a long time in many countries, the only two voices that have been heard have been the government or extremist groups. I am confident that the vast majority of people in the Arab world, as everywhere, are not extremists. What's important is to open up these systems so that other voices can be heard and people have a real choice to make. People need to have access to media and an ability to campaign and get their messages out. It's very difficult to judge the true strength of these groups in the current environment.

With blogging and internet connectivity on the rise, MEPI entered into the arena of youth cyberjournalism and cyberactivist training. MEPI earmarked resources to support NGOs to train cyberactivists in how to use communication tools and internet platforms for citizen journalism and democracy-promotion activities.

Alongside MEPI, the State Department was busy developing what it called "Diplomacy 2.0." Karen Hughes, the Under Secretary of State for Public Diplomacy and Public Affairs from 2005 to 2007, attempted to bring public diplomacy to the digital age. She established regional media hubs in Brussels, London, and Dubai with the intention of spreading news about US foreign policy in overseas broadcast media. She also initiated, somewhat controversially, a "digital outreach team" to monitor Arabic cyberspace and correct misinformation about US policies. But with a paltry team of only two, and a transparency policy that required the team to identify themselves as employees of the US State Department when they posted on Arabic sites, this initiative did not go very far. Nevertheless, these Diplomacy 2.0 initiatives, which involved partnerships with US embassies abroad, led to some novel synergies among diplomats, foreign embassies, local activists, and high-tech companies.

Take, for instance, the case of Wael Abbas, the pioneering Egyptian cyberactivist who was among the first people to use YouTube for anti-torture campaigns. In 2007, YouTube removed two videos documenting police abuse that he posted from his account. The videos were flagged for violating YouTube's community guidelines, which forbid videos with "shocking and disgusting" content. In all likelihood, a Mubarak-regime electronic militia organized the assault on Abbas's account. Abbas contacted YouTube directly to reinstate the videos, but to no avail. He then reached out to the US Embassy in Cairo and requested that they contact Google, which owns YouTube, on his behalf. The details of Abbas's request to the embassy appear in an embassy cable dated December 2007, which was made public by WikiLeaks. It reads:

Prominent Egyptian blogger, human rights activist and winner of the 2007 Knight-Ridder International Journalism Award, Wael Abbas, contacted us November 17 to report that YouTube removed from his website two videos exposing police abuses—one of a Sinai bedouin allegedly shot by police and thrown in a garbage dump during the past week's violence ... and the other of a woman being tortured in a police station. Abbas told us that YouTube is also preventing him from posting new videos, and he asked us for assistance in urging YouTube to re-post his removed videos and reinstate his access to uploading new material. Abbas said he has tried to contact Google, but has not received a response ... Abbas is an influential blogger and human rights activist, and we want to do everything we can to assist him in exposing police abuse. Abbas' post of a video showing two policemen sodomizing a bus driver was used as the main evidence to convict the officers in November 2007.

The cable ends with a specific request: "that the Department please contact Pablo Chavez of Google to try to resolve this matter." The intervention was successful. Abbas's videos were reinstated on his website and he resumed his anti-regime cyber-agitation.

The story, however, does not end there. Abbas's association with the US Embassy would come back to bite him. In September 2013, Abbas was one of thirty-five activists, including the founders of the 6th of April Facebook page, named in a complaint to the Egyptian public prosecutor. He was called in for questioning on suspicion of treason and working with a foreign government. The names of the activists were taken from a confidential US embassy memo from 2007 entitled "Outreach to Egyptian Democracy and Human Rights Activists," made public by WikiLeaks in August 2011. This memo details meetings with Egyptian activists from the blogosphere, civil society, and the opposition press. At the time of writing, the fate of those activists remains unclear. What is certain is that activists often risk their own security, credibility, and public standing when they are on record as working with the US government. Their contact with the US government can range from very superficial encounters, like attending a reception or receiving training from a third party funded by USAID, to more suspect activities like participating in closed-door briefings with US officials.

The case around Abbas illustrates some of the inherently problematic aspects of public diplomacy that targets young independent activists. This type of diplomacy operates with highly skewed power differentials, as it brings young people to the table of high politics without clear lines of accountability, rules of engagement, or protections. By the end of the Bush Administration, the State Department fully embraced the idea of working directly with young Arab activists in a policy of cyberdissident diplomacy (CDD).

In the last six months of the Bush administration, cyberdissident diplomacy moved to center stage with the appointment of James K. Glassman to the post of Under Secretary of State for Public Diplomacy and Public Affairs. Glassman came to the position with a four-decade-long career in journalism, publishing, business investment (he wrote three books on investment strategies), and public diplomacy. He served as a member of the Djerejian Group and was chairman of the Broadcasting Board of Governors, where he oversaw the operations of federally funded international radio and television networks, including VOA, Alhurra, and Radio Sawa.

In his first State Department press briefing in July of 2008, Glassman spoke boldly about the need for the US to win the war of ideas if it wanted to maintain its global hegemony. He used language steeped in war and militarism, speaking of his role as an "allied commander" overseeing America's "ideological engagement" with the world. He proclaimed:

Our mission today in the war of ideas is highly focused. It is to use the tools of ideological engagement—words, deeds, images—to create an environment hostile to violent extremism. That's our mission. We want to break the linkages between groups like al-Qaida and their target audiences.

This ideological war depended on recruiting young people, particularly young Muslims, to serve as the proxies of the US. Glassman explicitly asserted, "It is the fact that the battle is going on within Muslim society that makes our role so complicated and that requires that we ourselves do not do much of the fighting. The most credible voices in this war of ideas are Muslims." Four months later, Glassman laid the groundwork for the proxy war of ideas when he held another press briefing devoted to the launch of the Alliance of Youth Movement (AYM). Jared Cohen, the youngest staffer at Policy Planning, stood firmly by his side.

Before joining the State Department, Cohen distinguished himself as a young scholar and travel writer. In 2006, he journeyed throughout the MENA region and wrote about the state of young Muslims in his book *Children of Jihad: A Young American's Travels among the Youth of the Middle East* (2007). He was especially impressed with the online interactions of Iranian youth and the ways they embraced communications technologies. He wrote that the internet was "their democratic society." Cohen was among the early "tech evangelists," or "tech utopians," at Policy Planning, and AYM was largely his brainchild.

Gandhi, Martin Luther King Jr., and Coca-Cola

AYM was conceptualized as an internet initiative that would combat youth extremism and empower young people while simultaneously benefitting American business. AYM was not an entirely novel idea. It borrowed heavily from the Serbian group Otpor and its activist training wing, the Center for Applied Nonviolent

Action and Strategies (CANVAS), which was established in 2003. Otpor and CANVAS, though not by any means a creation of the State Department, were very much on its radar and received US government funding. The spray paint for those celebrated graffiti images that appeared all over Belgrade in 2000 was paid for by combined USAID and National Endowment for Democracy (NED) funds via the International Republican Institute. Most Otpor activists were unaware of the US funding until after the fall of Serbian president Slobodan Milosovic.

In her 2011 *Foreign Policy* article "Revolution U," Tina Rosenberg lays out how Otpor paved the way for a "postmodern" and "neoliberal" youth revolution. Unlike the revolutions of the twentieth century, the twenty-first-century neoliberal revolutions reinforce the values of a free market consumer culture. Ivan Marovic, the cofounder of Otpor and a former CANVAS trainer, explained that he viewed youth activism as a form of product branding: "Our product is a lifestyle ... The movement isn't about the issues. It's about my identity. We're trying to make politics sexy." Otpor blended concepts and tactics from social movements and product marketing. As elucidated by Rosenberg:

> If the organization took inspiration from Gandhi and Martin Luther King Jr., it also took cues from Coca-Cola, with its simple, powerful message and strong brand. Otpor's own logo was a stylized clenched fist—an ironic, mocking expropriation of the symbol of the Serb Partisans in World War II, and of communist movements everywhere.

The 6th of April Youth Movement would borrow the symbol of the clenched fist for its own movement and marketing.

CANVAS established an online portal to provide resources in multiple languages to activists around the world who sought to drive out their own dictators. Among their most circulated resources were the documentary videos *Bringing Down a Dictator*, about the fall of Milosevic, and *A Force More Powerful*, about non-violent struggles in India, South Africa, and the US during the civil rights movement. The site also carried translations of Gene Sharp's book *From Dictatorship to Democracy*. During the 2009 Green Movement in Iran, the Otpor manual about how to topple a dictator, "Nonviolent Struggle, 50 Crucial Points" (available in sixteen languages including Arabic and Persian), was downloaded 17,000 times in the country.[1]

AYM was to function in a manner similar to CANVAS by providing internet activists with the necessary tools, resources, and know-how to carry out successful nonviolent campaigns. In his press conference, Glassman cited two history-making social media campaigns that served as prototypes for AYM. The first was Egypt's 6th of April Youth Movement, and the second was Colombia's No More FARC (acronym for the "Revolutionary Armed Forces of Columbia"), also known as One Million Voices Against FARC.

Oscar Morales, an unemployed web developer, ingeniously adapted the tools and architecture of Facebook, Skype, and instant messaging to build a spectacularly successful transnational campaign against FARC, the military wing of the Colombian Communist Party, designated a terrorist group by the US. This citizen-initiated campaign culminated in massive demonstrations on February 4, 2008, when some fourteen million people took to the streets of cities in Colombia and around the world.

Glassman explained in a press conference that the State Department would bring top bloggers and cyberdissidents together with figures from the US government and the US business sector. The first AYM summit took place in New York on December 4–5, 2008, at Columbia University Law School, with delegates from over fifteen movements from around the world. Among the speakers and panelists were staff from the US State Department, Homeland Security, the Hoover Institute, and Freedom House, along with representatives from major communication and media corporations including AT&T, Google, and Facebook, as well as key new media strategists from the 2008 Obama presidential campaign. MTV live streamed the summit, which was hosted by Whoopi Goldberg.

From its inception, cyberdissident diplomacy contained a number of internal contradictions and puzzles. To begin with, AYM set out to partner with and train dissidents from countries that were long-standing allies with the US, including Egypt. During Glassman's press conference, a writer for the Associated Press, Matthew Lee, questioned him about how the State Department could support political dissidents from countries that were close allies. Lee asked:

> You mentioned a little bit of a problem of your involvement and the credibility of these groups. Have you given any thought to the flip-side of that? I mean, in … cases like Burma or Sudan, Darfur, the LRA, you know, this is all great, well and good and for the FARC, too. But then you talk about groups that are in Egypt and Turkey … those governments which are your allies—one of which is getting billions of dollars a year from the US … and the other one is a member of NATO—these governments may not appreciate your involvement in inspiring or in helping to create this network of people … that … in the case of Egypt [they could see] as a threat. Don't you run the risk of unleashing something here that is going to come back to bite you, especially with our allies?

Glassman responded like a diplomat, avoiding the prickly parts of the question:

> We are very supportive of pro-democracy groups around the world. And sometimes, that puts us at odds with certain governments … We are communicating and engaging at the level of the public, not at the level of officials. So you know, it certainly is possible that some of these governments will not be all that happy that—at what we're doing, but that's what we do in public diplomacy.

A plausible explanation as to why the US government would, on the one hand, support the Mubarak regime with regular military aid to the tune of $1.3 billion a year, and, on the other hand, ally with and train the anti-regime opposition, is because of the principle that "Good diplomacy is about playing all sides."[2] Today's dissidents may very well become tomorrow's leaders.

A second inherent flaw of CDD is that it forms alliances with individual dissidents without possessing sufficient local knowledge about who they are and how they are situated in their home society. CDD can inadvertently strengthen the wrong side, or even worse, deliberately choose to support a side that aspires to gain power in order to advance its own party and interests, not to promote democratic change in the country.

For example, in his briefing, Glassman announced that members of the 6th of April group would be attending the AYM summit, but that due to security concerns he could not reveal their identities. A US embassy cable dated December 30, 2008, and released by WikiLeaks on August 30, 2011, confirms the attendance of at least one alleged member from the 6th of April Movement. The cable reads:

> XXXXXXXXXXXX [name blocked out] expressed satisfaction with the December 3–5 "Alliance of Youth Movements Summit" in New York, noting that he was able to meet activists from other countries and outline his movement's goals for democratic change in Egypt. He told us that the other activists at the summit were very supportive, and that some even offered to hold public demonstrations in support of Egyptian democracy … XXXXXXXXXXXX was appreciative of the successful efforts by the Department and the summit organizers to protect his identity at the summit, and told us that his name was never mentioned publicly.

The 6th of April Movement, especially in its first two years, operated in an especially horizontal, leaderless manner, without any clear chain of command, formal structure, bylaws, or rules of membership. Anyone who so much as became a friend of the 6th of April Facebook page could claim to be a member of the group. In the case of Activist X, the founders and core members of the 6th of April Youth Movement have consistently denied claims that any of its members participated in the 2008 AYM summit. It later came to light in 2011 that the person mentioned in the cable was a young Egyptian named Ahmed Saleh. One of the cofounders of 6th of April, Ahmed Maher, issued a formal statement denouncing Saleh and charging that he falsely claimed to be a member and cofounder of the movement. Saleh allegedly worked with the movement only as an occasional Arabic-to-English translator, which brought him into contact with members of the foreign press.

Thirdly, AYM goes to great lengths to marry activism with consumerism, a prescription that essentially de-radicalizes, and even de-politicizes, politics. AYM is structured as a partnership between the State Department and US corporations working in high tech, advertising, youth media, and food and beverage service. AYM did not look to corporate America merely as sponsors. Rather, AYM's very model of politics and activism derives from the corporate model of marketing youth lifestyles.

It was Jared Cohen's idea to enlist Roman Tsunder, the founder of Access 360 Media, Inc., the largest online shoppers' network in the US, and Jason Liebman, the cofounder and CEO of Howcast Media, to AYM. Liebman, who is an investment banker and former Google employee, has a knack for monetizing the internet. Howcast Media markets itself on its website as "the best source for fun, free, and useful how-to videos and guides." The company's short, catchy, and youthful videos "will help you with pretty much anything you need to know about; from How to Bake a Cake to How to Survive an Alien Abduction."

Howcast Media, with the financial support of the State Department, developed a line of videos for internet activists about human rights blogging, civil disobedience, and social media campaigning. A sampling of these have titles like "How to Protest Without Violence," "How to Launch a Human Rights Blog," and "How to Be an Effective Dissident."[3] These videos, following the house style of Howcast, run a couple of minutes long and exude youthful energy. They are cast with attractive actors in brightly colored, casual, and trendy clothing. AYM, by packaging politics in a way that's fun, cool, and creative, tries to attract youth to adopt a brand of politics that is liberal, pro-business, and that reinforces the global system of power.

For all the alluring youth-friendly features of CDD, the policy was never altruistic. Cyberdissident diplomacy provided a means for the US to advance its "hard power" interests by drawing more people from strategically important regions onto American technology platforms. Different branches of the US government, from the Department of State, Department of Defense, and Central Intelligence Agency, have collected critical intelligence about societies through data openly available on public online platforms. The more hawkish features of CDD came to the surface in 2009 in Iran.

Internet Freedom: The Iran Factor

In the summer of 2009, mass protests erupted in Iran as a result of a disputed presidential election. Against all projections, the sitting president, Mahmoud Ahmadinejad, was declared the winner. The supporters of his opponent, Mir-Hussein Mousavi, whose campaign color was green, poured into the streets by the millions in what became known as the Green Movement. For a brief time, it seemed that the mass protest could lead to some form of regime change. But the Iranian government mercilessly cracked down on the protesters, and the movement eventually dissipated. During the peak of the Green Movement, tech-savvy Iranians inside and outside the country used text messaging, Bluetooth, Facebook,

Twitter, and YouTube to report on events and coordinate their movements on the ground.

In what has now become social media lore, Twitter was planning routine maintenance during the heat of the protests. Jared Cohen, evidently on his own initiative and without clearing it with his superiors, emailed Twitter creator Jack Dorsey, whom he had met on a trip to Iraq earlier that year. He asked Dorsey to postpone Twitter's scheduled maintenance, since it would shut down services during a crucial juncture in Iran. Dorsey agreed. The Obama White House evidently considered Cohen's intervention an act of foreign policy recklessness, and some thought he should have been fired. But his boss, Hilary Clinton, backed him up. He not only kept his job, but entered internet history.[4] Cohen's intervention made the list of the "Top 10 Internet Moments of the Decade," as drawn up by the Webby Awards. Also on the list were the launch of the iPhone and the Obama presidential campaign.

The English-language press started to dub Iran's Green Movement the "Twitter Revolution," just as it had done for the 6th of April protests in Egypt in 2008. For all the triumphalist and cyberutopian rhetoric about the role of Twitter and Facebook in Iran's Green Movement, State Department meddling in a popular reform movement potentially put people, especially young cyberdissidents, at risk. As Evgeny Morozov astutely remarks in *The Net Delusion: The Dark Side of Internet Freedom*, the Twitter angle fed perceptions about the web as being "some kind of a 'made in America' digital missile that could undermine authoritarian stability."

It remains unclear just how critical Twitter was to people on the streets in Iran; various accounts point to it being of marginal significance at best. However, Twitter undeniably served a valuable intelligence function for the US government. The CIA's Open Source Center (est. 2005), an intelligence unit that monitors forums such as Twitter, Facebook, chat rooms, and radio overseas, had been closely observing the situation in Iran and gained critical intelligence on activist networks and strategies during the movement.[5]

In July 2009, with the Green Movement still underway, it became evident that the practices associated with cyberdissident diplomacy were not confined to the State Department. The Adelson Institute for Strategic Studies of the Shalem Center in Jerusalem (est. 2007) established Cyberdissidents.org, a website claiming to support cyberactivists in the Middle East.[6] The director of CyberDissidents.org, Daveed Gartenstein-Ross, is a self-proclaimed counter-terrorism expert based in Washington, DC with close ties to the Zionist lobby. Cyberdissidents.org's highly polished and professional website makes no mention of the Adelson Institute. Instead, the website presents itself as a neutral platform, "a non-partisan group comprised of a diverse range of nationalities, religions and ethnicities" who are all united by "an ardent dedication to human liberty." A recurring feature of CDD, and politics in the digital age more generally, is how anonymity is used to disguise political actors and political interests. Many online platforms hide behind obscurities like "humanity" and "global peace."

Meanwhile, back in Washington DC, the buzzwords at Policy Planning in the post-Green Movement era were "cyber-repression," "internet circumvention technologies," and "internet freedom." In July 2009, the US Congress earmarked $50 million to support technologies designed to circumvent internet censorship, particularly in Iran and China. The program Haystack was developed to allow Iranians to remain anonymous online. It was later discovered that Haystack contained some glaring coding errors that may have put users at even higher risk than those who did not use the service. The US Senate also swiftly adopted the Victims of Iranian Censorship (VOICE) Act and allocated $1.5 million dollars to the Berkman Center for Internet and Society at Harvard University to, among other things, study Iran's blogosphere. The State Department also set up the Near East Regional Democracy

Program (NERD) to support projects dealing with research, training, and network-building about new media, technology, and internet freedom and their relation to human rights.

In her book *Consent of the Networked*, Rebecca MacKinnon reports in compelling detail about the government wrangling over control and allocation of funds for activist circumvention technologies. In Washington's divisive climate, business interests clashed and competed with lobby groups, and a Republican-controlled Congress conflicted with a Democrat-controlled State Department. In the midst of the Washington turf wars, bigger contradictions about internet freedom policy were left unexamined. As MacKinnon relates:

> Bizarrely, most of the people involved in the fight for Internet freedom funding said little and did nothing about a blatant contradiction: although US taxpayer money is being spent to help activists get around censorship, much of the censorship in North Africa and the Middle East is being carried out largely by North American software ... Moreover, the fight over circumvention funding only further distracted politicians, policy makers, media pundits, and journalists from the deeper question of what Internet freedom actually means.

With little time or effort devoted to deeper reflection on the underpinnings of internet freedom, the policy charged ahead. Under the tutelage of Anne-Marie Slaughter, Director of Policy Planning from 2009 to 2011, Jared Cohen and Alec Ross, the State Department's two tech experts, became enthusiastic proponents of all things 2.0: Civil Society 2.0, Diplomacy 2.0, possibly even Revolution 2.0 (which would become the title of Wael Ghonim's 2012 memoir on the Egyptian revolution). Ross—who served as a member of the Technology, Media and Telecommunications Policy Committee of Obama's presidential campaign in 2009 before heading the newly created Office of the Senior Advisor for Innovation and Technology (SAIT)—enthusiastically worked with Cohen to bring companies from Silicon Valley—Google, Facebook, Twitter, and YouTube, to name a few—to Washington, DC to sit at the table of high politics. As Morozov comments in his book *The Net Delusion*:

> Given the amount of research and technology money coming out of America's defense and intelligence communities, it's hard to find a technology company that does *not* have a connection to the CIA or some other three-lettered agency. Even though Google does not publicize it widely, Keyhole, the predecessor to Google Earth, which Google bought in 2005, was funded through In-Q-Tel, which is the CIA's for-profit investment arm.

On January 21, 2010, Secretary of State Hillary Clinton delivered what would become an iconic speech on internet freedom. The speech reiterated the US commitment to working with cyber-activists in closed societies to find ways around their governments' blocks and censorship. Clinton made numerous references to the two main strategic regions for US foreign policy: the Middle East and North Africa, and Asia and the Pacific. She made special mention of Iran, Egypt, Tunisia, Lebanon, Saudi Arabia, Pakistan, Afghanistan, Uzbekistan, Vietnam, and China. Clinton proudly announced that the State Department had been actively working in over forty countries with people who are "silenced by oppressive governments." Her office had been supporting these people by connecting them to other people in similar situations and providing a range of material and technical aid. She said:

> We are supporting the development of new tools that enable citizens to exercise their rights of free expression by circumventing politically motivated censorship ... [We are] providing funds to groups around the world to make sure that those tools get to the

people who need them in local languages, and with the training they need to access the internet safely.

Clinton stressed the importance of reaching out to Muslim youth: "The State Department has already begun connecting students in the United States with young people in Muslim communities around the world to discuss global challenges." In the question-and-answer session following the speech, she reemphasized: "In the wake of the President's speech in Cairo [on June 4, 2009], we have been expanding dramatically our outreach, particularly to Muslim youth." She was referring to a range of actions, from the appointment of Farah Pandith—a holdover from the Bush Administration—as Special Representative for Muslim Communities, to various global engagement (which is the State Department's euphemism for "Muslim programs") activities, which included Partners for a New Beginning.

From about this time, the "revolving door between the State Department and Silicon Valley" kept turning, to use a phrase from Morozov's 2010 *Foreign Policy* article. Jared Cohen left the State Department in 2010 at the behest of Google CEO Eric Schmidt to run Google Ideas, a "think/do tank," and to work on issues of counterterrorism and counterradicalization at the Council on Foreign Relations. His deputy at Google Ideas was Scott Carpenter, who ran MEPI in the final years of the Bush Administration. Cohen also cofounded the AYM offshoot Movements.org with fellow tech-evangelists-cum-venture-capitalists Jason Liebman (of Howcast video fame) and Roman Tsunder. Movements.org provides a wealth of resources for cyberdissidents, including a series of political Howcast videos. Jason Liebman notes in his bio on the Howcast site that of the over 100,000 videos on offer his personal favorite is "How to Smart Mob" because "it empowers youth activists and global citizens to use twenty-first-century tools to stand up against oppression."

"How to Smart Mob" is a two-and-a-half-minute video that

provides activists with step-by-step instructions for how to plan and get maximum publicity out of a "smart mob," a flash mob action used for civil disobedience. The video begins: "Want to get a point across in a very big way? Organize a smart mob, a group of people who mobilize on short notice to perform a collective action." The smart mob organizer needs only a plan, a computer with an internet connection, and contacts. He or she can then follow three steps:

Step 1: Determine your overall goal.
Step 2: Figure out the specific acts that will help achieve your goal.
Step 3: Prepare by scouting out location and getting contact information of people who plan to participate; can also organize through micro-blogging and social networking.

The video further instructs the smart mob organizer to "be aware of local laws regarding large gatherings. A smart mob could be illegal in certain instances." It advises participants in the smart mob to contact media in order "to publicize the smart mob action" and to "publicize photos and videos after the event" via social media.

The cyberdissident handbook produced by AYM/Movements. org is titled *Creating Grassroots Movements for Change: A Field Manual*. This practical how-to guide provides hands-on information that any aspiring cyberactivist would need in order to start and grow an online campaign or movement. For instance, Chapter 1 deals with "Getting Started." The first step is to "Choose your cause. Many movements begin in response to a particular incident." Step 2 advises, "Consider Names: A catchy name for your movement helps build your 'brand'." It continues with information on how to develop a mission statement, design a logo, and craft a message.

The manual is replete with practical advice and motivating statements. Above all, the blazing words of Oscar Morales, who built

No More FARC, the pioneering campaign in Colombia that got millions of people onto the streets, resound with the most force: "You must have a central motivator; a history, an event, a detonator which touches the fiber of people and is the hook by which people feel motivated to join."

From the time of that first AYM summit in 2008 that was inspired by the 6th of April Youth Movement, to the shifting of internet freedom from the margins of US foreign policy to center stage, Egypt was undergoing internal upheavals. The country plunged into a deepening economic crisis and unemployment rates escalated. Citizens battled increasing levels of police brutality and human rights abuses. At the same time, the young generation was getting wired at explosive rates. Amidst this pendulum of change, a young man from Alexandria was dragged out of an internet cafe and brutally beaten to death by two plainclothes police officers in full view of witnesses. His name was Khaled Said. He would become the detonator that would touch the fiber of the people and lead them on a path of revolt.

CHAPTER THREE

Marketing Martyrdom

The Martyr

On the night of June 6, 2010, twenty-eight-year-old Khaled Said enters Spacenet Internet cafe, just thirty meters from his home in the popular quarter of Cleopatra in Alexandria. Two men in plainclothes storm in and descend on Khaled like hawks. Despite their bulk, they move in synchrony and pounce on him. One of them clutches Khaled's collar while the other locks his arm around his waist. Khaled shouts and squirms to release himself from their grip, but in vain. They sweep him up and jerk him away from the computer terminals. One of them smashes his head against the marble countertop by the entrance. The cafe owner calls out, "No! None of that here." They drag him onto the crowded street and into the stairwell of a building two doors away. One grabs Khaled by his long hair and bashes his head against the marble wall. Khaled pleads with them to stop. The other man pulls out his pistol and clobbers Khaled over the head. Covered in blood, Khaled cries out, "Help me, I'm dying!" Neighbors hurry to the scene, some as young as twelve or thirteen, but they stand by helpless, watching in horror. A friend tries to intervene but gets pushed away. "It's none of your business motherfucker!" snaps one of the attackers. The more vicious of the two, the notorious officer Ahmed Othman, comes forward. Gruff and arrogant, he has a sadistic streak that is well known in the area. This is not the first time he has beaten his prey for sport. He kicks Khaled's body and it goes limp. In a moment of confusion, a doctor from the crowd steps forward. He lifts Khaled's arm to check his pulse, and somberly announces, "He's dead."

The attackers back off, somewhat shaken and hesitant as to their next move. They pick up the body, toss it in the back of a police truck, and flee the scene. A few minutes later they return and throw the body back in the stairwell, only to speed off again. An ambulance arrives at the entrance but the paramedics refuse to remove the body, not willing to interfere with a crime scene. One of them receives a phone call and then reluctantly lifts the body. Everything happened so fast. Not more than twenty minutes passed from the time of Khaled being accosted in the cybercafe to his body being transported to the morgue.

Khaled Said's death should have been just one more tragic foot-note in the annals of Egypt's Emergency Law. The thirty-year-old "temporary" Emergency Law extends the powers of the police while suspending due process of law and the constitutional rights of citizens. The Law, which goes up for renewal every three years, provides the legal basis for Egypt to function as a veritable police state. In 2010, Egypt's Ministry of Interior, the department which oversees State Security, had a staggering 1.4 million strong police force, nearly three times the size of the national army. Its mandate is to police the internal population, the "enemy within."

Martyr Makers

Since the early 2000s, a network of activists had been using online platforms to rally support to end the Emergency Law, raise aware-ness about torture in Egypt, and reform the electoral system to allow for competition at the level of the presidency. Khaled Said's death, in all its tragedy, quickly turned into an opportunity for activists working on these issues to galvanize youth into action.

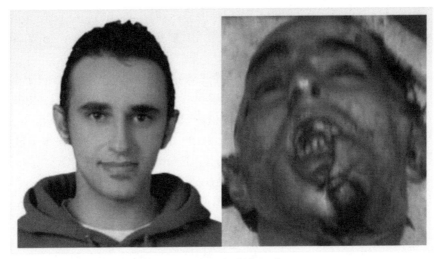

Figure 3.1: Before and after photos of Khaled Said

On June 7, the day after his death, two photos of Khaled Said entered Egypt's blogosphere and went viral. One was an airbrushed passport photo of Khaled with short hair and gentle eyes taken when he was a few years younger. His was the face of an everyday Egyptian nice guy, a regular *shaab* (youth). He could have been anyone's classmate, brother, son, friend, or boyfriend. The other photo, taken at the morgue by Khaled's uncle using a cellphone camera, depicts the bloodied, beaten, and mutilated face of Khaled, the latest martyr of the Emergency Law (Figure 3.1). These before and after photos sent shockwaves throughout Egypt's youthful cyber-spaces.

With the photos circulating widely, a story was needed to address questions that would inevitably arise about this Khaled Said person: Had he done something to get on the wrong side of the law? Was he another innocent victim of the Emergency Law? Three scenarios about what transpired that night outside the Spacenet Internet cafe circulated online and on the streets.

The first story came from a team of human rights lawyers from Cairo who, at the behest of Khaled's family, took on his case. They asserted that plainclothes police brutally beat Khaled after he refused to pay them a bribe. This initial explanation passed muster, since the police and security forces in Alexandria were notorious for extortion and violence.

The second story was the official governmental explanation from police and autopsy reports. According to this account, Khaled's death was caused by asphyxiation resulting from his swallowing a small parcel of marijuana to avoid arrest. Khaled could very well have been in possession of the drug. People in his neighborhood spoke of Khaled as a regular user of cannabis, a common practice among many of Egypt's youth. It is not a stretch to imagine that when confronted by police, Khaled may have tried to swallow incriminating evidence. Nevertheless, this scenario was ruled out by public opinion, since the image of Khaled's disfigured face did not support a story of death by asphyxiation, but by vicious beating.

The third rendering of that night's events originated from the blog of Ahmed Badawi, a member of the opposition Al-Ghad party. He earned his stripes as a pro-democracy activist when he was arrested in demonstrations on the 6th of April 2008. Badawy was the first person to post the before and after photos of Khaled, images that were quickly picked up by the Ayman Nour Facebook page and the online newspaper *Al-Youm al-Saba`a*. Badawi blogged that the police targeted Khaled because he had posted a video of a group of policemen dividing the spoils of a drug bust. Even though Khaled was not known among the community of bloggers and activists in Alexandria, the explanation of him as a brave citizen journalist picked up traction with "youth of the internet" (*shabab al-internet*). At the hands of seasoned activists, Khaled's life became a blank slate on which to write a compelling story.

The heroic narratives that circulated about Khaled held little resemblance to the actual person. In a richly investigated piece in *Jadaliyya* called "Saeeds of Revolution: De-Mythologizing Khaled Saeed," Amro Ali reveals that the image and life of Khaled Said

were "distorted almost beyond recognition." In contrast to the fictitious and idealized version of Khaled, the real-life person was a
young man living on the edge. He looked scruffy, was often seen
with a cigarette dangling from his mouth, and was known locally
not as an activist, but as a small-time cannabis dealer. He dressed
in gangsta hip-hop styles, struggled with long bouts of unemployment, hoped to immigrate to the US, and dreamed of finding love.
The life of the actual Khaled Said much more closely resembled
the struggles, hopes, and experiences of Egyptian male youth than
the martyr-activist Khaled.

If the story that circulated of Khaled's life was a fiction, then what
of the story of his death? The torture photo of Khaled's mangled
face shook a nation and would eventually shock the world. Yet there
remain doubts about the origins and veracity of this photo. Two
of Khaled's friends who were eyewitnesses to his death revealed
in interviews conducted for this book that when Khaled's body
was removed from the scene of the crime, his face was not very
badly disfigured.[1] It was bloodied, but not crushed and mangled
as it appears in the photo from the morgue. They conjectured that
perhaps the picture was taken following an autopsy. Maybe the
coroner cut open Khaled's face while trying to locate the packet of
cannabis the officers claimed he had swallowed. Another theory
is that the image was photoshopped. A forensic analyst consulted
for this book examined a low-resolution image taken from the
internet. He could not say if someone had tampered with the
image, since the quality was so poor. He did point to some suspi-
cious shadowing that could indicate it had been photoshopped,
but without an original photo, he could not make a conclusive
judgment. What is certain is that questions remain about the
morgue photo.

Egypt's youth of the internet accepted the activists' story about
Khaled Said at face value. They blogged about Khaled Said, posted
and reposted his photos, and a handful of people created Arabic
Facebook fan pages to him. One of those pages, "My Name Is

Khaled Mohamed Said," reached 70,000 members in its first day. A competing page, "We Are All Khaled Said" (*Kulina Khaled Said*), soon overtook it and would develop into one of the great experiments in social media history. This page would receive over 1.3 billion views in a span of six months and would be credited with triggering the most momentous revolt in Egypt in over half a century. The story of Khaled Said, and the Facebook page created in his memory, would become a thorn in the side of the authorities.[2]

The "We Are All Khaled Said" Facebook page (KS page) was created under the pseudonym "Elshaheeed"—The Martyr. The name was not chosen haphazardly. The concept of martyrdom (*shahada*) is deeply rooted in Muslim societies and carries profound emotional power. Their stories are typically used in struggles of jihad, of good against evil, of the righteous over the corrupt. Khaled, the "Martyr of the Emergency Law," was aptly cast on the side of the righteous, and the Emergency Law and its enforcers, on the side of evil.

Up until the start of the January 25 Revolution, the admin remained anonymous and was highly enigmatic. From the launch of the page, members consistently pressed Elshaheeed to reveal his identity and clarify his intentions. The page had its own FAQ (Frequently Asked Question) section, and to the question, "Who are you?" Elshaheeed responded: "I'm a regular Egyptian guy who supports Al-Ahly [football club] and who sits in cafes and eats *lib* [watermelon seeds] and who gets sad when the Egyptian soccer team loses." He explained how he needed to remain anonymous for fear of persecution.

Elshaheeed used the cover of anonymity to cultivate an aura of an "every-youth." This lack of specificity allowed members of the page to project themselves onto the admin, to see him as someone who shared their youthfulness, middle-class lifestyle, jokes, local knowledge, and emotions. An admin with an identity, a name, a face, a past, a location, known networks, and political associations would run the risk of repelling potential members. In mystery is unity. Yet for all of the admin's generic Egyptianness, Elshaheeed also carried unmistakable identity markers as a male and a Muslim, two identities that dominated the voice and culture of the page.

Unlike traditional political movements that unify members along lines of religious identity, political ideology, and charismatic leadership, the KS page pursued a deliberate policy of no leader, no politics, no ideology. The admin went to great lengths to distance himself from any political affiliation and to maintain a stance of independence. Elshaheeed repeated time and again that he did not belong to a political party, opposition group, or organized movement, and held no affiliation with a foreign government. He was just someone working with other volunteers after the death of Khaled Said to support torture victims and work against the Emergency Law and police brutality in Egypt. The launch and early activities on the page conveyed that this was no haphazard creation of amateur Facebook kids. This was a well-designed and calculated campaign with a mission.

The Brand

The cyberdissident manuals in circulation at the time of the launch of the Khaled Said page all underline the importance of naming and branding a social media campaign by using marketing techniques. The AYM manual, *Creating Grassroots Movements for Change: A Field Manual* published by Howcast in 2008, for instance, explains that

> A catchy name for your movement helps build your "brand." People who may know nothing about your cause will create an initial perception of who you are and what you stand for based on your name alone, so pick something that represents your beliefs and sounds like a call to action.

"We Are All Khaled Said" takes the collective "we" and brands it as a group—"youth of the internet" with a common identity and purpose. The brand's logo is the airbrushed photo of a clean-shaven Khaled, an everyday Egyptian, someone from a simple middle-class background.

The Launch

Any marketer knows how crucial the launch is for the success of a product or campaign. An expert such as Wael Ghonim, the Google marketing executive, took special care with the launch of the "We are All Khaled Said" Facebook page. Ghonim earned an MBA from the American University in Cairo in 2007. As luck would have it, Facebook became available in Egypt that same year. Wael's gusto for marketing was evident by his first footprint in Facebook land. On his personal Facebook page his earliest activities showed his fascination with advertising. He posted creative ads for cars, technology, and Pepsi. As he related in his memoir, "Learning the science behind marketing was key to my career progress, and later on was vital to my online activism … Little did I know that [it] would come in quite handy in promoting a product I had never seen myself marketing: democracy and freedom!"

He understood that the first key to a successful launch was timing. Internet-based companies draw on user analytics, consumer reports, and tools that track user trends to decide when to launch a new product. If you need your ad to get clicks, you aim to post it on a site with a high number of page views during peak traffic times. In the US, internet traffic is heaviest on weekdays because the internet is used for work. Traffic decreases significantly on weekends when people tend to go offline for their leisure activities. This pattern is reversed in the Arab world, where the internet has not reached high levels of integration into business platforms and infrastructure. It is mainly used for leisure and entertainment. Internet usage therefore goes up significantly on the weekends and in the evenings. The ideal launch for a promising marketing campaign in the Arab region is on the eve of the weekend. In Saudi Arabia, for example, the weekend begins Wednesday evening, since Thursday and Friday are non-working days. In Egypt, it's a day later, since Friday and Saturday make up the weekend. The admin made his calculations with precision and knew exactly when his target users, young Egyptians, would be online in the highest numbers—Thursday night. On June 10, 2010, the first Thursday after Khaled Said's killing, at exactly 9:01 PM, the time that marks the beginning of the weekend, the "We Are All Khaled Said" Facebook page went live. The initial posts were carefully calculated to attract the target audience and build the page's brand:

Post #1 (9:01 PM, Thursday, June 10, 2010)

Oh you inhuman: We will claim Khaled Said's Right[3]

I'm Egyptian. I will never accept Khaled's murder by torture, by heartless people with no mercy. These people were confident they could get away with murder because they're from the police. I'm Egyptian. I will not let the blood of this young man be wasted. I'm Egyptian like Khaled. The day they went and killed Khaled, I didn't stand by him. Tomorrow they will come to kill me and you won't stand by me. The person that killed Khaled and soiled his hands with Khaled's blood shouldn't see the light of day anymore. People like this do not deserve to live. They do not deserve to live in Egypt among us.

This initial post, which in marketing would be called the "pitch," uses the timeless narrative technique of setting up a clear-cut scenario of good ("we") versus evil ("you"). The message is sharp, unambiguous, and forceful. It begins as a national campaign with the words "I'm Egyptian," words repeated three times. It then sets out to polarize two groups, "I" (who is aligned with "we") and "you," the interlopers. The "you" points an accusing finger to not only the individuals who killed Khaled, but to all the "inhuman" ones who perpetuate a system that runs on torture, violence, and denying people their rights. The "we" are the Egyptian people, and more pointedly, the Egyptian youth. The pitch is supported with keywords that match the emotional and cultural references of the target audiences, words like "blood," "torture," "mercy," and "no heart." The pitch also tugs at the powerful emotions of guilt and fear with the words, "The day they went and killed Khaled, I didn't stand by him. Tomorrow they will come to kill me and you won't stand by me." These words are meant to galvanize the reader into action. The words "light" and "live" are used in connection to "us," the righteous. "They," the killers, the transgressors, should live in darkness, and not live among "us" good Egyptians at all. Finally, the post closes with a threatening message to the perpetrators of the crime. It stirs anger at the killers as it reinforces the good-versus-evil script that is a classic ingredient of holy struggle.

Post #2 (9:02 PM, Thursday, June 10, 2010)
It's our right and we won't give it up.

The word "right" that appears in the pitch is repeated in this second post to reinforce the (human) rights and justice angle of the campaign. The words "won't," "we," and "our" signify determination and unity. These small details are the ingredients of messaging that make for a successful launch and marketing campaign.

Post #3 (9:09 PM, Thursday, June 10, 2010)
[Five photos, one of the youthful portrait of Khaled, and four others of parts of his limp body in the morgue]

Post #4 (9:15 PM, Thursday, June 10, 2010)
The day they went and killed Khaled, I didn't stand by him. Tomorrow they will come to kill me and you won't stand by me.

A technique of television advertising is to shorten the ad over time. The cut-down segment isolates a core message of the longer ad. The same marketing practice appears in the fourth post. The admin singles out a melodramatic sentence from the initial pitch and repeats it a few minutes later. These words tear at the emotions of the reader in the attempt to compel her into action.

Post #5 (9:19 PM, Thursday, June 10, 2010)
Hey everyone, we are now 300 after a couple minutes. We want to be 100,000. We have to unite so that we can make a clear stand against the ones who oppress us and think they own our life.

In marketing, the ultimate goal is to drive up the numbers. Just minutes into the launch, the admin sets his target and assigns the members the job of growing the page themselves, presumably by posting links, tagging posts, emailing, and other means. Later in the day, the admin posts a video with the words, "This video must be watched by 10 million Egyptians." The focus on numbers and driving membership is an everyday part of a marketer's job, and the admin is pushing the right buttons.

Post #6 (9:42 PM, Thursday, June 10, 2010)
My blood is in your necks, [vindicate me] oh Egyptians.

The Martyr is resurrected from beyond the grave to endorse the campaign! He speaks directly and hauntingly to the people. The expression, "My blood is in your neck," carries a religious connotation, meaning that if a person does not take responsibility for stopping injustice, he will have to answer on the Day of Judgment.

Post #7 (9:52 PM, Thursday, June 10, 2010) [Khaled speaking]
The prosecution issued its initial report citing the cause of death as drug addiction and drug overdose. Isn't it enough that

**you killed me? And now you want to ruin my reputation … ?
You people with no conscience. May God be my witness, you
people with no conscience.**

Post #8: (10:02 PM, Thursday, June 10, 2010)
We are the ones who killed Khaled

　Khaled Said is a young Egyptian guy like millions of other ordinary Egyptians. He goes online, goes out with his friends. He lives
his life just like we do everyday. Khaled is one of us. He was no
criminal or troublemaker. He was a very normal young Egyptian
guy. But in just a flash, Khaled faced his destiny at the hands of
those criminal killers. It took only twenty minutes.

Branding begins here. The "us" in the words "Khaled is one of
us" brands Egyptian youth as a group—the *shabab* of Facebook
(Facebook youth). This term gets localized and Arabized and
becomes *shabab al-Face.* They are Egyptians who, like Khaled, go
online and live "ordinary" middle-class lives. And here the middle
class to which Khaled belonged is depicted as an urbanized and
somewhat folkloric middle class, as evidenced by his popular
neighborhood of Cleopatra situated along the Mediterranean in
Alexandria, and by his mother, who appears as a humble and traditional woman in her black abaya. The page operates solely in
Arabic, so it does not presuppose a bilingual or English-speaking
audience, but an "average" Egyptian one.

Post #9: (10:43 PM, Thursday, June 10, 2010)
**Next Saturday, in Alexandria, is the public funeral and prayers
for the martyr Khaled Said, in the Sidi Gaber mosque. A number
of national figures will be attending. We should definitely all be
there … Who's coming?**

The page functioned as a platform to capture and grow an audience online and involve it in campaigns for civil disobedience

offline. It took only one hour and forty-two minutes for the admin to call upon the page's members to get out into the street. This first call was for them to attend the funeral of Khaled Said, the "people's funeral." The post prompts members to respond by asking, "Who's coming?" This question is not simply rhetorical. By ending the post with a direct question, the expectation is that members will take action by either clicking "Like" or leaving a comment. In such a way, members of the page were constantly being pushed to participate directly in the cause.

Post #14 (3:44 AM, Friday, June 11, 2010)
6th of April calls for a demonstration, on Sunday at 5:00 PM in Cairo. Please everyone attend.

Take note of the timing. The admin worked around the clock to keep the launch alive. Also, take note of the fact that the Khaled Said case, which originated in Alexandria, was taken up in Cairo, the center of Egypt's activist community. The 6th of April Youth Movement, already well established on social media, immediately organized street protests in Cairo under its banner and was in communication and coordinating with the admins on the Khaled Said page.

Post #19 (11:53 AM, Friday, June 11, 2010)
Hey everyone, we have to get pictures of those animals who beat Khaled to death and spread them around the net ... these animals must pay. The officer Ahmed Othman and his assistant, Mahmoud Al-Falah, are responsible. These people should not sleep a night in a calm house.

The two policemen implicated in Khaled Said's killing became household names due to the efforts of *shabab al-Face* who collected, shared, and circulated information about them. The KS page borrowed the tactic of "naming and shaming" from fellow cyberactivists. Since roughly 2006, a number of bloggers have devoted their efforts to uncovering police brutality and corruption by publicizing names and posting photos and videos of torture. Instead of living in fear of police terror and accepting their roles as victims, these youth of the internet sought to invert power relations and create a situation whereby the police lived in fear of them.

Post #48 (2:06 PM, Saturday, June 12, 2010)
Down down with Hosni Mubarak, down down with [Interior Minister] Habib al-Adly.

"Down down with Hosni Mubarak" (*Yaskut yaskut Hosni Mubarak*) is a slogan that was put into circulation in 2004 by activists in the Kefaya movement. Most young people outside activist circles would not have dared chant these provocative words in public. By posting this opposition chant on its wall, the page positions itself as a fearless space. The KS page emboldens its members and pushes the boundaries of dissent, knowing there is power and protection in numbers.

With the launch off to a successful start, the admin was ready to flex his marketing muscle and take the page to the next level.

The Marketing

I cried for half an hour, I swear, when I saw [Khaled's] picture the day before yesterday. We are 50,000 and we are not going to leave Khaled.

—Elshaheeed, June 11, 2010

"Charisma" and "marketing" are not terms that normally appear together, but in the case of the KS page they are inseparable. Charisma, according to the *Modern Oxford English Dictionary*, is the "compelling attractiveness or charm that can inspire devotion in others." The admin developed a charismatic online persona that, combined with marketing dexterity and connections, proved to be a winning combination to grow the page's membership. By June 12, just two days into the launch, membership reached 50,000, halfway to the original target. Membership would climb at a rate the admin did not anticipate. After a mere five days, the page reached its target of 100,000. A week later, membership doubled. The pace of growth slowed temporarily, only to pick up again in November, presumably because of the November 2010 parliamentary elections.

The admin kept members motivated and involved in growing the page's membership by posting regular statistical updates. By November 2010, daily page views were over five million, a remarkable number by any account.

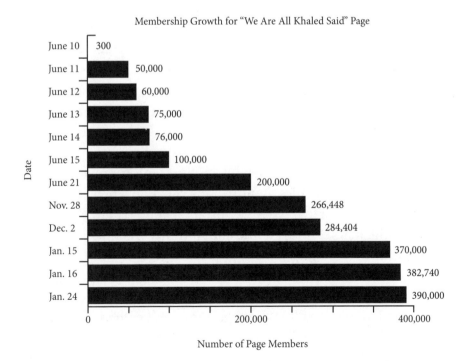

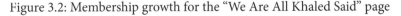

Figure 3.2: Membership growth for the "We Are All Khaled Said" page

Table 3.1: Membership growth for Khaled Said page (November 2010)	
Monthly Active Users	266,448
Daily New "Likes"	3,246
Daily Post Views	5,089,409
Daily Post Feedback	7,366

This admin understood the techniques of online marketing and used them in a highly consistent and professional manner, as seen in the pitch-perfect launch. The very first posting received 200 "Likes" and 910 comments, signs that traffic was immediately directed to the page. Online marketing campaigns hold certain advantages over traditional media marketing. With social media, users provide detailed information about themselves such as their age, sex, location, interests, education, family, and even their relationship status. Background information, combined with trends and data from users' clicks, subscriptions, memberships, times of access, and postings, is fodder for the online marketer, who uses this information to effectively target and spread the message.

Speed and scalability is another advantage of online marketing. A marketer can expand a campaign's target in a matter of seconds with just a few clicks. He can track in real time the effectiveness of an ad campaign by running analytics tools and watching live user data. This ability to track user interaction with campaign assets through detailed statistics about who is clicking, when, and from where, provides many types of instantaneous data. With such insights, the marketer can refine and optimize a campaign on the spot. Online marketing knows no boundaries. A campaign can target youth in Egypt with the same messaging, timing, and efficiency as any other online community in the globe.

To bring more eyeballs to the page, the admin embedded its URL on high-viewership YouTube videos about the KS torture case. And he paid attention to the details. He did not just post the URL as an amateur would, but shortened it to better fit in text. For instance,

instead of posting the long and cumbersome URL http://www.
elshaheeed.co.uk/home-khaled-said-full-story-background-
truth-what-happened-torture-in-egypt-by-egyptian-police/,   he
would convert it to a shortened form and post it as http://bit.
ly/8YR4LA. These details, though small, illustrate the technical know-how and thought that went into running the page. By
looking at traffic trends and membership jumps, the admin likely
pursued other strategies like publicizing the page on portals and
blogs, sending mass messages, or running search ads within
Facebook, Google, and Yahoo.

Professional marketing strategies aside, the admin connected
directly to this group's emotional, religious, and national psyche,
and this is where his charisma was important. When he writes, "I
cried for half an hour, I swear, when I saw [Khaled's] picture the
day before yesterday. We are 50,000 and we are not going to leave
Khaled," he establishes an emotional connection with members.
In high schools and colleges around Egypt, students were changing their profile photos to the image of Khaled Said.

The AYM manual advises leaders of social media campaigns
to form strategic alliances with people from human rights, religious communities, and opposition politics to lend legitimacy
to the campaign. The admin strategically aligned with the highly
regarded Nadim Center for Human Rights, whose lawyers were
working pro bono on the Khaled Said case. In an early post,
the admin wrote, "These are the real Jihadis. Everyone should
join their page." And in return, the Nadim Center endorsed the
KS page.

The single most important endorsement came from the
Mohamed ElBaradei Facebook page. ElBaradei, the former director general of the International Atomic Energy Agency (IAEA),
shared the Nobel Peace Prize with the IAEA in 2005. ElBaradei's
campaign was called the National Association for Change, and the
Facebook group that formed to help get him on the presidential
ballot became an online sensation. Over a quarter of a million

members, mainly young Egyptians, "friended" the page. ElBaradei had the fan base the KS page needed to take off. At exactly 9:06 PM on June 10, five minutes after the KS page went live, the ElBaradei page posted the following: "A message from the admins of ElBaradei's page: We invite all Egyptians to join the page of the Martyr Khaled Said who got tortured until his death by police in Alexandria." The "Point of No Return" traffic sign, an image that would become commonplace on the KS page and other campaign pages, accompanied the post.

The KS admin followed up a few days later by urging members to directly contact the ElBaradei admin: "Hey people, the Mohamed ElBaradei Facebook page has a quarter of a million people. Write their admin and ask them to change the page's profile picture to Khaled Said. Right now they're putting a picture against the Emergency Law. We want the picture of Khaled."

The ElBaradei and KS pages share a strikingly similar marketing style. Shortly after its own launch in February 2010, the admin of the ElBaradei page posted: "Yesterday we were 1600 members … today we became seven thousand … thanks to all who shared the page of Baradei fans. Please put the page link on your walls and also share the articles that get published here … We want to become 15,000 by Thursday."

Recall the post on day one of the KS page: "Hey everyone, we are now 300 persons after a couple minutes. We want to be 100,000." It would later come to light that Wael Ghonim was the admin in charge of marketing on the two pages. But for reasons that are not entirely evident, Ghonim denied publicizing the KS case on the ElBaradei page. He writes in his memoir *Revolution 2.0*: "The logical first idea was to publish news of Khaled Said's murder on Dr. Mohamed ElBaradei's Facebook page … but I reasoned that doing so would exploit an event of national concern for political gain."[4] Regardless of his claims, there is no doubt that Ghonim used the popularity of the ElBaradei page to direct traffic to the KS page, and the two pages worked to reinforce each other.

The Peace Brand

We're the shabab al-Facebook, really smart youth, youth who get it, youth who can totally keep our cool.

Our strength is in our silence.

On June 19, 2010, the *shabab* of Facebook descended into the streets to present their newly minted selves to the world. Their first fully self-organized event was a silent stand, their own version of a peaceful civil disobedience flash mob. The world had never seen anything quite like this: young Egyptians dressed in black, standing in lines that spread kilometers long in the cities of Alexandria, Cairo, and Mansoura. The admin enthusiastically wrote to members prior to the event:

> Do you know what the strength of this idea is? The main idea is that we are not an organization. We are not a party. We have no goal other than to express our opinion in a civilized way. Our strength is in the fact that we do not know one another and we aren't going to do a demonstration. No one will ask you, "why are you standing in this public place?" since you're not actually speaking to anyone. Imagine the media passing by the Corniche throughout Alexandria and filming the youth, their backs to the street. I swear, the entire world will talk about the *shabab* of Facebook!

During the silent stand the *shabab al-Face* stood still and somber, many reading the Quran or the Bible. They carried no signs, shouted no slogans. They remained peaceful and silent. It was not entirely clear to onlookers what this group wanted or why they were there. Their very presence irked the police even though they were technically not breaking any laws. They made sure to stand far enough from one another to avoid being charged with taking part in a political gathering, something forbidden under the Emergency Law.

Young women, even ones from conservative families and from small towns, proudly and courageously took part in the silent stands. They posted on the page and called on the boys to follow suit. An Egyptian woman by the online name of Emmy Cutty posted on the page at the start of the first silent stand: "[I am] standing on the Corniche you guys … come on, come down … I rode the train for 10 hours since yesterday to arrive to Alexandria … I am from Sohag and I came to stand with Khaled and his family … come on now."

The Facebook youth had been well instructed ahead of time to maintain their cool: "If a policeman provokes you, don't reply, act as if he's not even there." When police predictably tried to disperse the silent standers by shouting at them or jabbing them with batons, the *shabab al-Face* did not react. After an hour, they dispersed, by walking away in different directions without a word. They would return in the coming weeks for second, third, and fourth stands, repeating their message to end torture and the Emergency Law.

The silent stands were a key element of the page's brand, and the admin worked hard to defend its trademark. When a member wrote a comment that ridiculed a picture from one of the silent stands, the admin wrote: "Guys. Anyone who makes fun of any picture in the member pictures folder will be kicked off the page. [This will happen] after one warning and the chance to delete the comment … you'll be kicked off the page even if you were an active member."

A good marketer does his best to control his brand, but at the same time needs people and the media to spread the word and advertise the product. Step 4 of the AYM manual urges:

> Use the press: Figure out your outreach strategy: The more people hear your message, the more influential you'll be. Contact the media—print, radio, television, online—whenever possible to

tell your story. If a sympathetic foreign dignitary or organization happens to visit, try to meet with them, or organize a protest to coincide with their arrival, which can get you some international press attention.

Through crowdsourcing, the page started formulating its media plan as early as June 14, four days into the launch. The admin wrote:

> Hey everyone, tonight our plan is for all of us to call the talk shows. Please, can people send us the telephone numbers so we can use these in our [media] plan? We want you to find the numbers of all the talk shows in Egypt.

He would soon mobilize members to help him build a more comprehensive database of bloggers, journalists, and television personalities with reach in Egypt, the region, and internationally.

Exhibiting a high degree of preparedness and planning, on June 14, the admin also publicized the first draft of the page's media strategy: "Plan to Contact Media on the case of Khaled Said, First Draft." It used more numbers and marketing techniques to motivate members: "[We are] 100,000 … If 10 percent of us calls the shows, we will get our voices heard … these TV programs are watched by millions of people."

Bloggers and journalists became well acquainted with the entity Elshaheeed, who pursued them relentlessly via instant chat and email messages (from Elshaheeed@gmail.com). A well-known blogger recounted the first time the name Elshaheeed popped up in his instant chat box.

> ELSHAHEEED: Hey, U there? Love your blog :)
> BLOGGER: thanks. do I know you?
> ELSHAHEEED: probably not :) unless you are on the Khaled Said page.
>   R u?

BLOGGER: I am ... Oh wait ... are you the admin??

ELSHAHEEED: yep. And I need your help :) We are organizing a silent stand next Friday. Can u attend and blog about it? help us spread the word ... we need to stop these criminals.

The blogger obliged, as did so many others who were contacted, charmed, and cajoled in a similar way. The silent stands received a good deal of local and international news coverage. Stories about the *shabab al-Face* appeared on the *Huffington Post*, in the *Washington Post* and the *New York Times*, and locally in the Arabic papers *El Dustur*, *Misr Inaharda*, *El Masry El youm*, Al Jazeera online, and RNN, to name a few. The editor-in-chief of *Al-Youm al-Saba`a* went as far as to say, "The influence of the [Khaled Said] Facebook page is stronger than the Ahram newspaper [the #1 daily semi-official newspaper in Egypt]."

The admin constantly repeated that the page was not a political party or group:

We are not a party, we are not a movement, and we are not a group ... we are any optimistic Egyptian, guy or girl, who got together to demand our rights and the implementation of law. We don't want anyone to use our cause for their own political gains ... we have to remain one voice ... a voice that no Egyptian would disagree with ... a voice that demands the rights granted to us by our constitution and Egyptian law.

The admin controlled the KS image and the page's message through carefully crafted press releases and the FAQ section. The response to the question "What do you want to achieve?" read as follows:

Our main and only goal is to end torture in Egypt. We do not have any hidden political agenda nor do we get any support from any organization. We have the support of thousands of individuals both Egyptians and International supporters. This is what we need: support from individuals worldwide—no one else. We also want to show the world that Egyptians are standing up for their rights. Brave Egyptian men and women, along with their brave international supporters, will no longer stay quiet about torture in Egypt and Police brutality and we will expose everyone who commits or condones torture.

Who could possibly refuse to help young people with such focused and noble goals? A critical mass of sympathetic media personalities eagerly promoted The Martyr's page, clinching the marketing campaign and upping membership numbers exponentially.

ELSHAHEEED: Ok. Great! Thanks I gtg

BLOGGER: Oh wait ... Aren't you going to tell me who you are??

ELSHAHEEED: I am ElShaheeed :)

And in a click ... he's gone!

CHAPTER FOUR

Virtual Vendetta

On January 25, 2013, the two-year anniversary of the start of the Egyptian revolution, a group called Black Bloc appeared on Egypt's streets for the first time. These figures, clad from head to toe in black, moved through the streets in packs and had the distinctive look of video-game or comic-book characters. Many wore the iconic Guy Fawkes mask from the film *V for Vendetta*, and some donned black hoodies with the words "Fuck the System" on them. As they swarmed through Cairo and Alexandria, they formed human shields and obstructed roads, bridges, train tracks, and government buildings. For the most part they did not carry weapons, though some had Molotov cocktails stuffed in their pockets. More importantly, they were armed with the idea that together, anonymously, collectively, they could wreak havoc on the system, bring it to a halt, and even bring it down. A rebel culture rooted somewhere between fantasy and anarchy had been spreading and mutating in Egypt for some years. It took form in football stadiums, in the virtual spaces of the "We Are All Khaled Said" page, and on the streets.

From its inception, the membership of the Khaled Said page included an anarchistic and virtual-fantasy strain. The demographics of the page tilted young, with 70 percent of members under the age of twenty-four. They constituted a generation who had grown up in front of screens, with video games, and inside virtual spaces. Whereas one of the page's admins was thirty-year-old Wael Ghonim, a professionally trained marketer who moved within the Google corporate establishment, the other admin was twenty-three-year-old AbdelRahman Mansour. He embodied a kind of homegrown Arab virtual hero. Since the age of seventeen Mansour had been involved in some of the most pioneering and popular youth initiatives on the Arabic web. He has said, "For me the internet, technology, is like water. It's part of anything I do in my life."[1] It is as if for him the internet contains the essence of life itself.

Up until the start of the January 25 Revolution, the "We Are All Khaled Said" page embodied a duality. The page vacillated between espousing a message of pacifism and silent civil disobedience—as in the wall message that said, "Hey guys, when you're on the streets don't move an inch no matter what the police do to you"—to one of confrontation and bellicosity, as in this post: "The head of the person that killed Khaled and soiled his hands with Khaled's blood shouldn't see the light of day anymore. People like this do not deserve to live. They do not deserve to live in Egypt among us." The two sides coexisted in a symbiotic relationship. On the flip side of any mask of pacifism is often a mask of menace. And on the Khaled Said page, that mask took the form of the anti-hero V from *V for Vendetta*.

V for Vendetta began as a comic book series by Alan Moore and David Lloyd. It was adapted into a film in 2006. The story, set in a dystopian totalitarian Britain, serves as a warning to governments not to try to push their people too far into submission. The antihero V survives a personal ordeal of captivity and torture and dedicates his life to taking revenge on his captors. He also awakens his fellow citizens to recognizing their collective power. After taking control of state broadcasting, he persuades them to rise up against their government. V is inspired by Guy Fawkes, the mastermind of the foiled Gunpowder Plot of November 5, 1605. The aim of the plot was to blow up the British Parliament, an act immortalized in

Figure 4.1: *V for Vendetta* at Ahly vs. Zamalek match, December 8, 2009

the famous quote "Remember, remember, the 5th of November." V dons a mask in Fawkes's image and rekindles his plan to blow up Parliament. Among other things, V is a pyromaniac and expert maker of explosives. The name "V" stands for "vendetta," "vengeance," "victim," "villain," "victory," "violence," and "veritas," but it should also stand for "virtual," since in the lead-up to Egypt's revolution V came to signify the anonymous virtual warrior.

The iconography of *V for Vendetta* entered Egypt's rebel youth culture via a local ultra soccer group in 2009. From there it moved into Egyptian virtual spaces. During a December 8 match between arch rival teams Zamalek, home to Ultras White Knight (UWK07), and Al-Ahly of Ultras Ahlawy (UA07), the White Knights hung a massive banner of V with the words, "Remember, Remember, the 8th of December." The ultras relish spectacle and regularly set up elaborate banners and firework displays at their matches. It is no wonder that V, the dramatic arsonist, anarchist, and torture victim, appealed to ultras.

Ultras loathe the corporatization of their sport and have a strong anarchistic streak. A slogan of the global ultras is "Football is for you and me—not for fucking industry." Egyptian ultras are staunchly anti-system, anti-police, and pro-games. In the words of "Bouka," an Ultras White Knight, they are "PlayStation geeks."

After the fall of Mubarak in February 2011, and during the temporary rule of the Supreme Council of Armed Forces (SCAF), the ultras were at the forefront of violent showdowns in the cities. A Facebook post by one of them shows how they bring the world of games to the streets:

> The SCAF don't know that we are the generation of PlayStation and video games. Hey SCAF, before you take over the authority of Egypt, know that we were killed thousands of times every day till we won the battle with the monster. We never get bored. We can spend hundreds of years to complete all the levels of the game. And believe me, we will do it.

Similar comments appear throughout ultra Facebook pages. Following a street battle in 2012, an ultra protestor wrote, "We will get a big score, I'm sure. It's [like playing] Mario again, how nostalgic. It seems that the SCAF didn't play Resident Evil."[2]

The ultras are an unpredictable political force. They exhibit a high degree of group discipline and can mobilize quickly. When they make an appearance on the political stage, they do so almost as a social organism bonded by a common culture of video games, football, and anarchy. They delight in political theater and exhibit a high-voltage energy and physical discipline as they single-mindedly confront their adversary. They wear masks and costumes, recite slogans and sing their signature songs, and jump and move in unison in a choreographed way as they wave their banners and release fire into the night with Molotov cocktails and fireworks. Ultras sometimes direct their energies against "the system," yet at other times it manifests as violence against each other—the other team.

They seem to have no attachment whatsoever to ideology. Their lack of ideology makes them vulnerable to manipulation, to being unwittingly led into fighting other peoples' battles. Though they lack ideology, they do not lack a set of ethics by which to live. Ultras reject the commodification of their culture and are big advocates of volunteerism. They refuse to take money and profit from their activities. They also reject individual media pres-tige, opting instead to be identified as simply "an ultra." During the eighteen days that made up the first phase of the revolution, and then again during the second phase in November 2011 on Mohamed Mahmoud street, the ultras took on the security forces and suffered scores of deaths as a result. In February 2012, their battles took a different turn following a football match in the city of Port Said. Rival fans faced off against each other in a deadly confrontation that resulted in seventy-nine fatalities and over one thousand injuries.

Ultras were among the crowd of youth who congregated on the "We Are All Khaled Said" page. They were the page's rabble-rous-ers, itching for some real street action. V stood as their model for revolt.

From Football Land to Virtual Land

When *V for Vendetta* moved from Egypt's soccer stadiums into the virtual realm, it spread deep into the arteries of the KS page. The KS page's earliest nod to V was on June 14, 2010, just four days after its launch. The admin embedded a five-minute film, "Khaled for Vendetta," on the page's RSS feed. A second, albeit less imaginative film, "Khaled Vendetta," was posted on the page's own YouTube channel, TheShaheeed, on July 29, 2010.

The creator of "Khaled for Vendetta" was Mohamad Alim, a writer, blogger, filmmaker, political activist, and member of the 6th of April Youth Movement. He wrote on his blog that the par-allels between *V for Vendetta* and Egypt under the Emergency

Law were so glaring and natural that he produced the film in just half a day.

The film opens with ominous music from *V for Vendetta*, followed by a fade-in and -out of Khaled's image over a black backdrop. The shot cuts to a session of the Egyptian Parliament (*Majlis al-Sha'ab*) on May 11, 2010, with the then Prime Minister, Ahmed Nazif, announcing the renewal of the Emergency Law for two more years. He proclaims that it will be used only to confront drugs and terrorism. Members of parliament applaud. The words "drugs and terrorism" echo several times.

V sets down the first domino.

The next scene opens with a homemade film of a smiling Khaled in what appears to be his bedroom, followed by the now infamous morgue photo of his mangled face. There is a close-up of a newspaper clipping reporting that under the auspices of the Emergency Law, two plainclothes police beat Khaled Said to death. The masked man stacks more dominos.

The shot moves to a scene from the original film, a conversation between two police investigators, Finch and Dominic, about how everything is connected:

> FINCH: I suddenly had this feeling that everything was connected. It was like I could see the whole thing; one long chain of events that stretched back … I felt like I could see everything that had happened, and everything that was going to happen. It was like a perfect pattern laid out in front of me and I realized that we were all part of it, and all trapped by it.
>
> DOMINIC: So do you know what's gonna happen?
>
> FINCH: No. It was a feeling. But I can guess. With so much chaos, someone will do something stupid. And when they do, things will turn nasty. And then, Sutler [the leader] will be forced to do the only thing he knows how to do. At which point, all V needs to do is keep his word. And then …

In the meantime, V is setting up an elaborate pattern of dominos in the shape of an encircled V. He flicks the first domino and sets off scenes of violence, chaos, destruction, fire, protests, shouting, upheaval—all clips from Egypt. Within the chaos are flickers of people who presumably can emerge to build a new Egypt. They include Mohamed ElBaradei and Abdelmonem Mahmoud, the Al Jazeera journalist and ex-member of the Muslim Brotherhood who was jailed in 2007 for reporting on torture.

The film ends with two still images. The first is of police surrounding, in hugely disproportionate numbers, a small group of demonstrators. The second shot depicts people outnumbering and surrounding the police. This closing image conveys the film's dictum that "People should not be afraid of their governments. Governments should be afraid of their people."

The YouTube video blurs reality and fantasy. It conveys an emotionally charged message to the viewer about the need to revolt against the Mubarak regime and provides visual instructions about how to do so. The deft dialogue conveys a set of ideas about the power of the people. Short locally produced YouTube films of this sort that circulate widely on popular pages like the KS page give the independent filmmaker the role of imaginer of the nation, writer of a new historical narrative, and creator of a path for the future.

The viewer comments posted in Arabic and English on YouTube illustrate the extent to which the spaces of social media were mixed and plural. The range of positions represent Mohamed ElBaradei supporters, pious Islamist-oriented youth, anarchists, and supporters of the Mubarak status quo:

Brilliant video ... Maybe Dr. El Baradei will be our 'V' here in Egypt to save us ... God bless you

Beneath this mask there is more than flesh. Beneath this mask there is an idea, Mr. Adly [Interior Minister], and ideas are bulletproof.

First of all ... do u think that is a proper method to deal with what we are living and sinking in now ... Believe me guys not the chaos will be the way to get rid of our present ... This video misleads u although i don't know the person who did that great job but the result will not be the way ... By the way I'm not belonging to the democratic party [NDP, party of the Mubarak regime] and not even think to join it ... But i belong to my country (Egypt) and think that changing the case starts with us.

Great video ... may God bless you, brother Mohamed. I'm going to ask God to deliver you from this crisis soon. [Fifteen "Likes"]

Thumbs up! what an amazing video and maybe chaos will be there sooner or later! May Allah bless u.

As V entered more deeply into Egyptian popular culture, he was Egyptianized. For instance, in a cartoon posted on the KS page in

Figure 4.2: "We seek God's aid to help us through misery," July 29, 2010

July 2010, V holds a sign in Arabic that reads "We are All Khaled Said." In the background are the pyramids, the Cairo Tower, a church, a mosque, and the Nile. The scene depicts a person—a symbol of Egyptian youth—drowning in the Nile next to a capsized boat. The caption reads: "We seek God's aid to help us through misery." God and V are called upon to bring justice to Egypt.

In his memoir *Revolution 2.0*, Wael Ghonim mentions in passing the presence of *V for Vendetta* on the KS page. He takes credit for bringing V into the virtual realm, yet at the same time Ghonim goes out of his way to defang V politically. He writes,

> In 2006 I had seen the movie *V for Vendetta* and fallen in love with the idea of the mysterious warrior fighting against evil. I was still influenced by this idea when I created the Facebook page ... I identified with V's desire for change, although in no way did I approve of his violent means.[3]

The character of V, who embodies vengeance and violence, complicates Ghonim's branding of the page as a nonviolent campaign. Ghonim has always been squeamish about politics to the extent that he even frowned upon protesters chanting anti-Mubarak slogans. He was clearly no ultras sympathizer. In actual fact, Ghonim worked as part of a two-person team running the page. His contribution was more on the side of marketing, branding, and media outreach, whereas the "other admin," Abdelrahman Mansour, seven years Ghonim's junior, was much more steeped in creative Arab rebel youth culture.

Unmasking the Other Admin

I swear to God that after witnessing the dogs of the internal ministry torture, beat, and violate people's honor I can never be silent again. This is it. I have become more determined than ever to defend the rights of an entire people who are becoming enraged :'(((((((((((
                                                    —Elshaheeed, June 23, 2010

AbdelRahman Mansour exemplifies a new breed of activist. He comfortably and unapologetically traverses different groups and ideologies and refuses to be pinned down to one current. He is at home with liberals, Islamists, anarchists, leftists, Christians, Marxists, ultras, agnostics, environmentalists, Arabs, and non-Arabs. He observes and absorbs new ideas and perspectives as he seamlessly moves between the virtual and physical worlds.

A native of Mansoura, AbdelRahman grew up between Egypt and Saudi Arabia, where his father worked as a financial manager and his mother as a high school biology teacher and principal. Mansour attended his first street demonstration in 2003 with his parents, both long-time members of the Muslim Brotherhood, to protest the invasion of Iraq. In 2005, the year of Egyptian parliamentary and presidential elections, he joined the Kefaya movement and entered the arena of anti-Mubarak activism. He enrolled in Mansoura University as a business major but soon switched to his real calling, information sciences and journalism. As a college freshman Mansour and a group of friends produced a satirical and radically anti-Mubarak political magazine entitled *Town Guys (Awlad El Balad)*. They printed and distributed five thousand copies around campus, to the great scorn of State Security, who chased students around in an attempt to confiscate all copies. Mansour recalls, "This was my first real journalism experience. At that time I got detained for one day at the State Security, but they didn't interrogate me. They said, 'He's a guy from Kefaya so let's leave him alone so no one complains.' So, they let me go." The next time State Security captured him he did not get off so easy. He spent three days in jail for filming a demonstration during the local elections and suffered a harsh beating. He felt helpless and humiliated: "I felt like if I had power in my hands I could have answered the humiliation."

In 2004, while still in Saudi Arabia, Mansour worked with the enormously popular preacher Amr Khaled on his website, magazine, and television program *Life Makers*. He went on to write and blog for the online newspaper *Al Arabiya*, where he established himself as an emerging voice of the Arab youth opposition and gained a growing following of readers. In 2006, Mansour joined a group of bloggers in one of the first Arabic citizen journalism websites, Al Jazeera Talk, a youth initiative created by Al Jazeera. Al Jazeera Talk awarded Mansour a scholarship to travel to Darfur, Sudan for a month in November 2008, where he investigated the civil war there and learned about war blogging and reporting. At the young age of twenty he carried out exclusive interviews with the vice president and assistant vice president of Sudan.

With the arrival of Facebook in the Arab world in 2007, Mansour immediately took to experimenting with the limits of social media. He used the status update feature as a political, personal, and poetic space. His earliest status updates were lamentations about Egypt. On August 11, 2007, the twenty-year-old Mansour wrote: "I'm weeping on your hands, but I try to sing. I know that I am a country, but I'm exiled and I am not myself. I try to sing when I am weeping." The following month he invoked martyrdom, a trope that would become a trademark of his virtual activism: "This air has become very heavy with the stench of bodies. The martyrs disappear to hide the truth of their killers."

Other posts were more audaciously anti-Mubarak. Between 2007 and 2008 Mansour's posts included "END MUBARAK'S CORRUPTION," "Down with the president forever. Not because he's immortal but because he has a son [to take his place]," and "Oh Mr. President. Damn you and the Emergency Law!" In his most audacious updates he wished death on the president. "Burn Hosni, burn today or tomorrow," and "I wish Hosny Mubarak diiiiiiiiiiiies!" He took his anti-Mubarak stance to even higher levels when he created an anti-Mubarak Facebook page with another friend. They called the page "Mubarak Passed Away" (*Mubarak Matt*). Mansour saw this page as a form of dark political humor as well as an experiment to test the boundaries of social media activism: "We were trying to create something fun and test people's reactions." A total of 744 people were daring enough at the time to "Like" the page.

For a year and a half Mansour was an active member of the Muslim Brotherhood and worked on its official Arabic and English websites, the latter known as Ikhwanweb. In 2009, after the Muslim Brotherhood published its new political platform, Mansour and a group of friends made the decision to break with the group. They specifically objected to the Brotherhood's position that neither women nor Copts should be eligible for the Egyptian presidency. In an effort to try to retain its young members, the group elders arranged a meeting between Mansour's group and the head of the Brotherhood's political section, who at that time was Mohamed Morsi (the same Morsi who would go on to become Egypt's first civilian president after the revolution). But he could not persuade them to remain in the group. Apart from its discriminatory platform, Mansour experienced the Brotherhood as too hierarchical and out of touch with the lives and concerns of its younger members. He explained, "I can't say there was one single reason for leaving the group, there were several reasons. I wanted to be part of a broader movement, something bigger than the Brotherhood. I wanted to continue working [politically] but not necessarily by belonging to one party or a single organization."

Mansour branched out to work with a range of independent online platforms and global civil society movements. He was a contributor to the annual Arab feminist blogger event organized by We are All Laila (*Kulina Laila*), where he started championing women's causes. He participated in the transnational activist network Global Voices, working for a time as a translator supporting the cause of internet freedom. He took part in Greenpeace in support of a project that promoted wind turbines as an alternative energy source to oil. Mansour went on to cofound WikiLeaks Arabic in 2010. He exhibited an intuition for finding and working with timely causes and for articulating the "voice of the Arab youth."

Mansour's ability to articulate the youth position proved especially effective in the lead-up to Obama's visit to Cairo on July 5, 2009, when Obama delivered a historic speech about Islam which essentially won him the Nobel Peace Prize. Mansour authored an article for *Al Arabiya* on May 30, 2009, entitled "Ten Tips for Obama Before His Visit to Cairo." The article became a political manifesto signed by hundreds of Arab youth. In the article, Mansour chastised Obama, and the US more generally, for supporting Mubarak and Arab authoritarian regimes, in contradiction to all the pro-democracy rhetoric:

> Choosing Cairo is a generous reward for the Mubarak regime, which has not succeeded in the past 25 years in holding even one truly democratic and fair election … If you [Obama] fail to critique Mubarak and the despotic Arab regimes you would extinguish hope in the promises you made in your inaugural speech to support democracy and political reform in the Middle East.

To further hone his skills as a virtual activist, Mansour participated in intensive courses on civil disobedience and strategic planning sponsored by the Academy of Change (*Academeyet el Taghiir*). He became good friends with one of its founders, Wael Adel. In an interview with the author in 2012, Wael Adel talked about the kinds of people they hoped to reach through the Academy:

> We initially didn't have specific youth in mind, but we were hoping for people like AbdelRahman. A page like "We Are All Khaled Said" was extremely important for spreading our ideas. I can't claim the page is based on our ideas, but it played a key role in spreading them. The same goes for the 6th of April page. When I see these pages posting words like "It's our generation's right to

try ... to present an experience from which the next generations can learn," I feel good because this is the exact slogan we used in the Academy of Change website a few years back. So it's not like we were telling anyone what to do, or directly feeding them ideas. They took ideas from us and decided themselves what to use and spread.

Mansour was inspired by the Academy's literature about non-violent civil disobedience and the importance of changing the mentality of people through what the Academy calls a "mind-quake." He watched and shared news about the Academy's recommended films, which included *The Matrix*, *Battle in Seattle*, *Hitler: The Rise of Evil*, *Gandhi*, and *V for Vendetta*.

The film that held the greatest influence over Mansour was *Battle in Seattle* (directed by Stuart Townsend, 2008), about how protesters stopped the meeting of the World Trade Organization (WTO) in Seattle in 1999. He recounted:

This movie was very inspirational for me and it really affected my life. I watched it about forty or fifty times. It really impressed me when the demonstrators were able to stop the meetings of the WTO. I mean, it's impressive when regular people can convince the big powers of the world to stop a decision. Countries exist and governments exist, but at the end of the day there is something else; there is the person with a human life. What happens at the end of the story? Human beings leave the government to take the side of humanity. I am taking the side of humanity. Even if you don't want to call it anarchy, call it something else. But I am on the side of the human beings. People should be the main source of power in the world, the source of inspiration and change.

Mansour's open-mindedness and global thinking made him a natural fit for the Mohamed ElBaradei National Association for Change campaign in early 2010. He ran ElBaradei's official

Facebook page with Wael Ghonim in what was their first collaboration. Mohamed ElBaradei's brother Ali later joined them as a third admin. Mansour saw ElBaradei as a unifying figure, the kind of leader who could bring a more humanistic and global dimension to Egypt's fractured and stagnant political culture. ElBaradei offered an alternative to the two political choices between Islamists and the military. Mansour explained:

> ElBaradei spent a big chunk of his professional life working against one of the greatest threats faced by humanity—nuclear weapons. The existence of these weapons means that at the end of the day a million people can be standing in a place and a missile could kill them. It's extremely disturbing to think about how people can lose control over their lives as machines take that control. One of the main reasons I support ElBaradei is because he has been challenging the nuclear armory.

Mansour is committed to working towards a society where force, weapons, and state violence are reduced to the lowest possible degree. In 2010 he was planning to launch a police monitoring website called Police Watch. The goal was to create an "internet government" by the people to monitor security forces and police at three main sites: checkpoints in the streets, police stations, and public universities. The plan was to create a Twitter hashtag that any citizen with an internet connection could use to tweet and report their encounter with the police, whether good or bad. The admins of the site would use a crowdsourcing mapping application to monitor where high numbers of violations were taking place. Police stations that respected people and the law would be rewarded with good ratings, whereas the abusers would be publicized and subject to citizen action.

As plans were underway for Police Watch, the Khaled Said incident took place and diverted his energies. Mansour recalls:

I was very affected by Khaled Said. Once I saw him I instantly identified with him. I said this could be me, exactly. I used to go to
cybercafes just like Khaled. He was killed in the street just outside
the cybercafe … When I first saw his face I was shaken for days,
I couldn't take it. I never imagined such a thing could happen to
someone like him. I was aware that when it comes to the police, all
people are the same. We're all vulnerable. But I never thought this
kind of violence could reach that degree with a citizen.

Immediately following Khaled Said's death, Mansour met
with several activists and bloggers from the Kefaya movement,
the Muslim Brotherhood, and the 6th of April Movement. They
wanted to do something, to use the incident as a way to mobilize society. Mansour, with his experience and knowledge of the
Arab cybersphere, and Ghonim, with his online marketing deft-
ness, decided to work as coadministrators on their own Facebook
page—the "We Are All Khaled Said" page—and the collaboration
made history. Mansour did not consider himself the leader of a
movement in the traditional sense. He viewed himself as a citizen,
"a citizen who lives on the internet."

Mansour spent up to twenty hours a day on the KS page in its
first three months. He was so consumed by his work on the page
that he completely neglected his studies. When his friends asked
him what he was doing online all the time, he would tell them,
"I'm preparing for the revolution." He added, "I was being sarcastic, of course. So what happened? A revolution happened. An
actual revolution!"

In actuality, Mansour had harbored hopes for an Egyptian revolution and publicly spread the idea of revolution in ways that
turned out to be eerily prescient. In a 2008 article he wrote for Al
Jazeera Talk, Mansour envisioned the scenario of a future Egyptian
revolution:

An army general, a state security officer, and their security forces stand in Tahrir Square, the main and largest public square in Egypt. They observe the square where traffic has come to a standstill … The general orders his soldiers to fire teargas on the crowds who have come to protest against poor living conditions. As the canisters fall in all directions, people run forward and then retreat, taking the teargas canisters and hurling them back. They have occupied the parking area where they hold a sit-in on the big square.

They chant, "We want freedom and bread! We want justice and security. We can't stand torture and impoverishment any longer! We hate our wardens and oppressors! We hate our big prison and our ongoing imprisonment. Shed light on our nation with freedom and renaissance, with justice and security, with dignity and respect for human rights" …

We will soon meet the [great] Egypt of the past in our future. This new Egypt will undergo a renaissance of freedom and hope. We will share these experiences with the entire world.[4]

Deviating from the Script of Silence

Early in the life of the KS page, the Khaled Said youth were packaged as a peaceful, non-ideological, and a non-political entity. Their silent stands were a feat of online-to-offline mobilization. But just weeks into performing their silent stands, the crowd became impatient. The admin planned the fourth silent stand for July 23, 2010, the date commemorating the 1952 Egyptian Revolution/military coup against the Egyptian monarchy. As a nod to the historical significance of the date, this event was dubbed "The Revolution of Silence." Some members—ultras and activists from the 6th of April Movement among them—were fed up with the admin's insistence on repeating the silent stands. On the day of the event, they decided to march to the home of Khaled Said in the district of Cleopatra in Alexandria, where they chanted, "Down, down with Hosni Mubarak!" (*yaskut yaskut Hosni Mubarak*). They also joined together in another chant initiated by the ultras against Habib al-Adly, the reviled Interior Minister. In typical ultras fashion the chant was a play on words. In Arabic, "habib" means "loved" and "adl" means "justice." The chant *walla Adly walla Habib…irhal ya w`azir il-tahzib* means "neither Just nor Loved…go away you minister of torture."

Ghonim, who was administering the page remotely from Dubai, was upset when he learned that the Khaled Said youth went into anti-Mubarak mode. He writes in his memoir:

> I was a little angry at the activists. It was not as if I liked Hosni Mubarak, but I did not want to lose the support of those page members who would find a direct attack on the president to be either inappropriate or very risky, or to create a conflict between the page members who held different opinions; the page had to do its best to stay focused and gather people around the cause.

As much as Ghonim wanted to contain the Khaled Said youth and have them stick to a behavior commensurate with the brand, the community who made up the movement moved on multiple fronts. The group morphed from a collectivity of silent protesters into a movement with its own politics, codes, and rebel culture. The Khaled Said page and movement took on a life of its own: it was not entirely leaderless, but not exactly led. Members took pride in knowing they were part of a virtuous society that stood apart from the corrupt society of the outside adult world.

The virtual wall of the Khaled Said page testified to the duality of a movement which supported both peaceful and confrontational forms of protest. It displayed figures like Gandhi, Martin Luther King, and Gene Sharp, who reinforced the script of nonviolent civil disobedience. These figures coexisted with V and Malcolm X, who advocated for more assertive and combative methods.

In late August of 2010, a Malcolm X poster made its way onto the wall with the quote "Nobody can give you freedom. Nobody can give you equality or justice or anything. If you're a man, you take it."

The comment below the poster reads:

> Very strong words from Malcolm X. Who knows him? He was one of the black Muslims in America who was among the strongest advocates for black rights and their equality with the whites … He said, nobody can give you your freedom or your rights. "If you're a man you take it." In this group we say, a man or a woman will take your rights, because women are more than half of the members of the group.

Malcolm X reemerged in December 2010 as the Khaled Said youth were making preparations for their revolution and his image became the profile photo of choice for scores of Facebook youth.

By the winter of 2010, the Facebook youth were getting restless. Growing numbers of Khaled Said youth balked when the admin called for yet another silent stand. The group was mutating further away from the media-friendly image of peaceful, dignified, silent youth, into a group that was more impatient, enraged, and darkly creative. This mood showed itself in December 2010 when a series of ghoulish, blood-colored e-greeting cards hit the walls of the page. Some members had designed cards to commemorate the upcoming Police Day holiday on January 25. These cards came straight out of the horror genre. In one card, the words "Happy Holidays to Men of the Police" were superimposed over a photo of a lone man about to be clobbered by a band of riot police. The cards also displayed faces and bodies of torture victims, alive and dead, around the iconic image of Khaled Said's mangled face. The Khaled Said youth planned to send these blood-curdling cards to police en masse for Police Day.

While the Khaled Said youth were sharing designs for their horror cards, Mansour was watching an unexpected uprising taking place in Tunisia. In a private chat with Ghonim at 3:05 AM on December 26, 2010, Mansour wrote:

> MANSOUR: Are you following the news from Tunisia? It's the Egyptian scenario
> GHONIM: no
> MANSOUR: [Link to story about demonstrations from Sidi Abu Zeid in Tunisia] We should do something
> GHONIM: it's good but not now. Let's wait to see what happens in Tunisia. Because if it's a sad ending it will be against us.

On December 28, Mansour raised with Ghonim the question of organizing something for Police Day. They had a private chat at 5:12 AM:

> MANSOUR: I will make an event, a demonstration against the Police on January 25.
> GHONIM: Let's think about it. It's a Tuesday!
> MANSOUR: It's a formal holiday.
> GHONIM: Are you sure it's a formal holiday?
> MANSOUR: yes, I'm sure and you can check this link from Wikipedia

They often settled questions with a link to a news article or Wikipedia entry.

In a plot borrowed directly from *V for Vendetta*, Mansour proposed a nationwide march for January 25. The idea was for people to appropriate the police holiday and march on the Egyptian Parliament. They would demand new elections, the dissolution of parliament (which stubbornly continued to renew the Emergency Law), call for the disbanding of State Security, and insist on the resignation of Interior Minister Habib al-Adly. Before they had a chance to carry out their plan, an unforeseen event occurred that stunned the country and diverted the group's energies and attention.

During a worship service on New Year's Eve 2010, a bomb exploded at the Church of the Two Saints (*al-Qadaseen*) in Alexandria. It resulted in twenty-three tragic fatalities and scores of injuries. This devastating "holiday bombing" traumatized the Christian community and horrified the nation. The bombing also led to an unexpected new martyr of the Emergency Law, thirty-year-old Sayed Bilal. Following the explosion, which was supposedly carried out by a suicide bomber, State Security rounded up a number of suspects who were members of the Salafist group Salafi Front. Sayed Bilal was picked up on January 5, allegedly tortured to death by five officers, and died on January 6, prompting a demonstration of hundreds of people. Bilal has since been cleared of any involvement in the church bombing. On January 7, the Khaled Said page began posting images of the dead Sayed Bilal, in a style similar to how it posted the morgue photo of Khaled Said. The admin wrote, "We must understand well that the rights of Sayed are like the rights of Martina, Maryam, and Mina [Christians who died in the bombing]. All of them are Egyptians and it's not acceptable that any one of them dies in the way they did."

The admins condemned the church bombing in clear terms. However, the decision to take up and highlight the case of Sayed Bilal over the victims of the church bombing showed a deep insensitivity to the perspective and vulnerability of the country's Christian minority. The more the page advocated for the rights of Sayed Bilal, the more it opened itself up to criticisms and speculations that it harbored Islamist leanings.

Despite concerted efforts to market the story of Sayed Bilal in a way similar to Khaled Said, the victimhood story and body of Sayed Bilal did not inspire nearly the same degree of emotional response and sympathy. In photos of him, including the photo of his dead face, the salafist Sayed Bilal had a stern expression and a thick, long beard. Unlike the youthful image of Khaled Said with his soft eyes, slender frame, and youthful hoodie, Sayed Bilal's body was bulky, he wore Salafist garb, and he had a cold look. This image did not resonate with the young, non-Islamist-oriented population among the Facebook youth. Even a photo of Bilal holding his small child failed to lighten his image. Judging from their online posts, the young Salafists in the community tried to turn Sayed Bilal into a symbol for all the mistreatment they suffered at the hands of the Mubarak police state. They tried to construct Sayed Bilal as the new martyr who could rouse people to revolt.

In the midst of these tumultuous events in Egypt, a mass uprising was brewing in Tunisia, sparked by its own celebrity martyr, Mohamed Bouazizi. On January 13, 2011, twenty-eight days into the Tunisian revolt, an image of two hands symbolizing Tunisia whispering into the ear of Egypt appeared on the wall of the Khaled Said page. It included these words: "From the people of Tunisia to the people of Egypt. We hope the message arrives from Tunisia to bring freedom. In Tunisia the oppression is worse than in Egypt. Even though a large number of websites were blocked, tens of thousands of people still went down to the streets."

On Friday, January 14, 2011, President Zine El Abidine Ben Ali, after twenty-three years of sitting at the helm of Tunisia's police state and kleptocracy, boarded a jet and fled the country. He allegedly carried with him $60 million worth of gold bullion from the country's central bank. The unexpected and astonishing story of Ben Ali's exile spread around the Arab world at breakneck speed via all known means of communication, with Facebook being a key source of news. The image that immediately circulated on Facebook pages throughout Arab countries was that of V with the Tunisian flag in the background.

With the knowledge that the Tunisian people toppled their dictator, the youth of Facebook were unstoppable. They were determined to revolt. Despite attempts by authorities to threaten, cajole, and otherwise dissuade them, it was too late. Because, as V himself pronounced, "Beneath this mask there is more than flesh. Beneath this mask there is an idea … and ideas are bulletproof."

CHAPTER FIVE

Viral Revolution

On January 14, 2011, the trending Facebook status update for scores of Egyptians was "congratulations" (*mabrouk*), or simply "Tunisia." If the opening words in the launch of the "We Are All Khaled Said" campaign were "I'm Egyptian," after January 14 they would have undoubtedly been "I am Arab." The events in Tunisia rekindled the spirit of Arab nationalism and memories of the victory of the revolution on July 26, 1956. For a moment it was as if Gamal Abdel Nasser's vision of a united Arab people, the "Arab dream" (*al hilm al-Araby*), was coming to life.

Even as they were bubbling with admiration for their Arab brethren in Tunisia, Egyptians could not help but show some pangs of wounded national pride. If small Tunisia, with its population of 10.5 million, could succeed in bringing down its reviled president-dictator through a popular uprising, then why couldn't Egypt, "Mother of the World" (*Oom al-Dunya*), with its 85 million people, do the same? The admin, under the name of The Martyr (*Elshaheeed*), prodded Egyptians, especially the men among them, to follow Tunisia's lead: "There are people praying and hoping that Egyptians don't turn into real men … they are convincing themselves that what [the regime] did to us for over twenty years will keep us scared and frightened and hopeless … our simple response to them is four letters: t … u … n … s [Tunisia]." The Arab activists on Facebook, "*El-Face*," had to think on their feet and write their own playbook. The social media manuals for cyberdissidents offered no tips for what to do in the event of an actual regional uprising.

A small but vocal group of members on the Khaled Said page balked at the sudden attention paid to Tunisia. Some objected to how people were speaking about a fallen Arab leader in a celebratory tone, while others thought Egypt was not ready for it's own uprising. The voices on the page mirrored the rift within Egyptian society, which was split along lines of "pro-revolt" and "no-revolt." Polarization occurred not only between the pro-Mubarak and anti-Mubarak camps, but also within the opposition Muslim Brotherhood. Within the Brotherhood, the divide was largely along generational lines, with the elders being opposed to revolt on the grounds that they were not adequately prepared, whereas the younger members were ready for action.

In this politically charged moment, the admin of the Khaled Said page ran a survey to solicit member views as to whether they should turn their attention to Tunisia. A resounding majority replied in the affirmative. The admin responded:

> We will talk about Tunisia because 86% of you want us to do so … and this is not only to support them [Tunisians] in their fight for freedom and dignity … but also for people here to understand what's happening there. We should learn and benefit [from the example of Tunisia] to be able to answer the pessimists who say there is no hope.

On January 15, the admin made an intriguing proposition to turn Police Day into a day of protest: "Today is the 15th [of January 2010]. January 25th is the Police Day (*Eid al-Shorta*), an official holiday. If we get 100,000 people in Cairo onto the streets no one will be able to stop us. I wonder, can we?" That question drew 1129 "Likes" and 487 spirited comments and conversations. A sampling of comments, at times sarcastic, comical, worried, angry, indifferent, pessimistic, and fervent, illustrates that a critical mass was ready and willing to try for their own uprising:

LIDYA: We caaaaaaaaan, of course. And I'm telling you, I'm a girl and I'm going to be the first one dooooooooooooown.

SARA: No because I have an exam. looooooooooool

MAGDY: This is biiiiiiiig talk

HAMDY: You motherfucker you're a terrorist for real, I swear

HEMA: From the first hour this page was created I was saying we have to do a revolution and I know the admin probably remembers me very well ... Thank God that the [admin] is finally convinced that what was taken by force can only be recaptured by force.

EL SHERBENY: Is a revolution what you have in mind?

MICHAEL: No, we can't. We will back down and go back to sleep. We will get scared when we see a couple of people wearing uniforms or see the plainclothes [police] and we will say, "I have exams and my mom didn't let me go down."

HEAVEN SNIPER: Finally you're getting convinced ... but let's stop the bullshit of these silent stands. Starting today the silence must come to an end.

MOHAMED: Why don't we just send a text message to the Ministry of Interior and tell them about the timing and location of all this.

MOHAMED: This needs real MEN!

AHMED: The government is holding this country with an iron fist and I don't believe we can do what the Tunisians did. There was a time when we were the example and all the Arab countries looked up to us. Let the past return, the Orabi Revolution and the July Revolution.

MASRY HURR (A FREE EGYPTIAN):
The question: Tunisia
The answer: Tunisia
The start: Tunisia
The model: Tunisia
The manhood: Tunisia

The admin duly set up a Facebook event called "Revolution of the Egyptian People" (*Thawrat Shaab Misr*). In a single day, the invitation reached more than half a million Egyptians on Facebook, with twenty-seven thousand people confirming their attendance. Traffic to the Khaled Said page soared. On January 16, 2011, the page received 9,125,380 hits and membership rose to 382,740.

The "January 25 Revolution" was AbdelRahman Mansour's idea. His coadmin, Wael Ghonim, initially hesitated. Ghonim believed in brand consistency and had branded the page as a peaceful, nonpartisan, anti-torture campaign. He contrasted the brand of "We Are All Khaled Said" to that of a competing Facebook page, "My Name is Khaled Mohamed Said." The latter was, in Ghonim's words, "rebellious, angry, sometimes ill-mannered, and often dogmatic." Ghonim tried to dissuade Mansour from deviating from the page's script of silence, but the force of history and the roar of the people won the day. Ghonim eventually went along with the January 25 Revolution event, which was coordinated by a coalition of activist youth groups. They never thought in their wildest dreams that the "Revolution event" would trigger an actual revolution. In the best-case scenario, they thought their event could provoke a large-scale protest.

To persuade members of the page to take part in the January 25 protest, the admin used a tone more akin to a self-help motivational speech than to revolutionary zeal:

> The whole thing is easy I swear … the idea is that each one forgets the negativity, forgets the fear, and goes down from his house on January 25th with one goal … with the goal that we show them that we are hundreds of thousands of enraged Egyptians … we are not 10 or 20 or 1000 or 2000 … they have to understand that we are the majority, not the minority. Come on, let's show them our strength as youth.

In the lead-up to January 25, the Khaled Said community of predominantly high school and college students found themselves grappling with a host of complex issues pertaining to martyrdom, suicide, and poverty. At this moment of genuine deliberation, they struggled to find their collective voice and ethical positions.

In both Tunisia and Egypt, the tragic story of a young man-turned-martyr became the trigger for revolt. In Tunisia, Mohamed Bouazizi doused his body in kerosene outside a municipal building and set himself ablaze. In Egypt, plainclothes police officers beat Khaled Said in view of neighbors. These two men became symbols of mass movements, the detonators which touched the fiber of people and the hooks that motivated them to join, as the anti-FARC campaigner Oscar Morales wrote about in the AYM manual for cyberdissidents.

Activists have long understood the power of symbols in galvanizing people to join a movement; think of what Rosa Parks meant to the civil rights movement, or Nelson Mandela to the anti-apartheid struggle. In the age of social media activism, the difference has been that an image and story can proliferate in the guise of a meme and travel across space at breakneck speed. In the breathtaking pace at which images and stories spread, there is little time for fact-checking, reflection, or bottom-up movement building.

The meme-like spread of Mohamed Bouazizi seems to have traveled a path via social media similar to that traversed by Khaled Said. First was the grippingly tragic story of the martyr's demise. Bouazizi was a twenty-six-year-old man from Tunisia's interior region of Sidi Bouzid. He left high school early to work full-time in the informal economy as a fruit and vegetable vendor. As the eldest son in his family, he provided the primary support for his widowed mother and five younger siblings. Overwhelmed by the burden of fines, debts, and the humiliation of being serially harassed and beaten—in the end by a female police officer who literally struck the final blow to his dignity when she slapped him in public—he sought retribution. He tried to lodge complaints with government authorities, but they were indifferent to his plight. He became despondent. On December 17, 2010, on a public sidewalk outside the municipal building where he sought but never received justice, he set himself on fire. He died on January 4, 2011, from wounds resulting from his self-immolation.

Just a few hours before dousing himself in inflammable liquid, Mohammed Bouazizi supposedly wrote a suicide note that his cousin posted on his Facebook wall. The note, addressed to his mother, read:

> I'm traveling mom, forgive me, don't blame me. I'm lost in a road and have no control. Forgive me if I disobeyed your words. Blame the times, don't blame me. I'm going to a place with no return. I did not cry. No tear was shed from my eyes. There is no reason for blame. Blame is no longer useful. Time betrays its people. I got fed up … I gained awareness and I forgot all about the past. I'm traveling and I hope the reason for my journey won't be forgotten.

The note made its way from the cousin's Facebook wall through the Arabic blogosphere and onto the virtual wall of the "We Are All Khaled Said" page. Questions have been raised about the authenticity of this note. Some on social media have asked, "Did Bouazizi actually write this note? Or did someone else script this emotional note to stir sympathy and outrage in young Arabs?" We cannot answer these questions with any certainty, but we can doubt.

Bouazizi's mother staged a protest in front of the governor's office on the spot where her son committed his act of self-immolation. She supposedly cried out, "Where have you gone, men of Hamama?"[1] This method—of women calling to men to prove their manhood—would be repeated many times over in the lead-up to the various Arab revolts. A cousin of Bouazizi videotaped the protest with Bouazizi's mother and the footage landed in the hands of cyberactivists. This mother would come to symbolize the "mother of the nation," and after that, the "mother of Arab revolutions," in a way similar to what Khaled Said's mother represented for Egypt. As Bouazizi's story spread, it triggered protests throughout Tunisia. On January 14, 2011, President Ben Ali and his wife, Laila Tarabulsi, reviled for their nepotism, extravagance, and brutality, fled the country. Tunisia ignited the wave of popular uprisings that came to be known as the "Arab Spring," with Bouazizi as its symbol.

Mohamed Bouazizi's act of self-immolation, just like Khaled Said's death, could have faded into oblivion. Instead, these two figures became the national and regional rallying cries for people to rise up against their governments. The questions that beg to be asked are: To what degree did behind-the-scenes actors craft and package Bouazizi in an attempt to fuel popular dissent? And to what extent did Bouazizi's story go viral as the result of spontaneous and genuine citizen outrage and action? It is impossible to know the precise balance of spontaneity and planning, but some degree of deliberate and calculated intervention factored into the success of the Bouazizi-triggered uprising.

In an article titled "How Tunisia's Revolution Began," Yasmine Ryan recounts a tale that involves two male relatives, a mother, a peaceful protest, Facebook, and Al Jazeera:

> In Sidi Bouzid … locals fought to get news of what was happening out, and succeeded. Rochdi Horchani—a relative of Mohamed Bouazizi … helped break through the media blackout. On December 17, he and Ali Bouazizi, a cousin of Mohamed Bouazizi, posted a video of a peaceful protest led by the young man's mother outside the municipality building. That evening, the video was aired on Al Jazeera's Mubasher channel. Al Jazeera's new media team, which trawls the web looking for video from across the Arab world, had picked up the footage via Facebook.[2]

What the author left out of her account was that the satellite station, Al Jazeera Mubasher, does not operate as a neutral and objective television platform. From its very inception Al Jazeera Mubasher, the live Arabic segment of the channel, has been a barely disguised Muslim Brotherhood platform and mouthpiece.

Indeed, since the 1990s the Muslim Brotherhood has been swift to capitalize on media and communications liberalization to spread its messages and influence. Media commentators have long pointed to an alliance between the Qatari government, which funds and hosts Al Jazeera, and the Muslim Brotherhood. As reported by political commentator Sultan Al Qassemi, "Al Jazeera Arabic's bias toward the Muslim Brotherhood goes beyond the TV channel and is readily found on its website ... What Al Jazeera Arabic viewers end up with is nothing less than blatant propaganda for the Muslim Brotherhood."[3]

Just days after Mubarak's fall, a twenty-four-hour channel in Egypt, Al Jazeera Mubasher Misr, was launched. A spate of independent correspondents began leaving the channel, claiming it had turned into a mouthpiece for the Brotherhood. For instance, in December 2012, the correspondent Samir Omer explained in an interview with the German paper *Frankfurter Allgemeine Zeitung*, "I could not stand it anymore. This is no longer an Al Jazeera office. This is an office of the Muslim Brotherhood." The Muslim Brotherhood (MB) influence at Al Jazeera Arabic was something of an open secret until the time of the 2012 presidential elections in Egypt, when the MB decided to put forward Mohammed Morsi as its presidential candidate. At that time the group barely tried to conceal the fact that Al Jazeera Arabic was working in the service of the Brotherhood. By publicizing the Bouazizi story, the station was in all likelihood actively trying to fuel the already existing anti-government sentiments in the country, with the probable aim of paving the way for Islamist rule in Tunisia.

Notwithstanding the propagandistic slant of Al Jazeera, segments of the Tunisian population had been developing a grassroots oppositional political culture for years through online blogs and groups. In a 2004 report by the Arabic Network for Human Rights Information Gamal Eid described Tunisia as "The First, The Worst," meaning it was the first country in the Arab world to get the internet in 1991, and it had the worst record of human rights abuses related to internet activism.[4] The Tunisian state practiced draconian forms of cyber-repression. The Ben Ali government made it an offense to so much as visit a website determined to be a security threat or critical of the government. One could land in jail for the "unauthorised use of an Internet connection."[5] Such punitive measures gave birth to an opposition cyber-culture heavy with rebellion and dark humor. In this repressive climate, the dissident website TuneZine published a sinister joke: "TuneZine is launching a competition for jokes, reserved for young people, about Ben Ali and his party. First prize: 13 years in prison. Second prize: 20 years in prison. Third prize: 26 years in prison."[6]

It was no laughing matter when the admin of TuneZine, Ettounsi, was jailed and tortured for his online activities, showing that even jokes carry treacherous consequences. Segments of Tunisia's cyber-citizenry built a grassroots movement to tackle cyber-repression. In 2003, a group of Tunisian activists started a petition protesting the arrest and torture of forty internet users and the death of twenty-three-year-old Maher Al Asmany. The petition stated, "40 young Tunisian men have been jailed, sentenced to long terms and tortured, just for logging on to some websites claimed by authorities to be terrorist websites." The activists called for human rights advocates and civil society to make it a goal in 2003 to work towards achieving freedom of expression.

Despite the regime's ruthless and well-known policies around internet use, Tunisia was nonetheless chosen by the UN to host the second World Summit on the Information Society in November 2005. Reporters Without Borders issued a cutting press release with the title "The 2005 World Summit on the Information Society in … Tunis: Someone's got to be joking!" Robert Ménard, secretary-general of Reporters Without Borders, declared, "It is quite inappropriate, indeed outrageous, to hold this summit in one of the countries most hostile to the free flow of information … It harms the credibility of the summit's organisers and above all insults the spirit of the Internet, which is supposed to be a place where freedom reigns."[7]

Despite protests, the summit took place in Tunisia from November 16 to 18, 2005. It resulted in the Tunis Commitment, a protocol agreed upon by "representatives of the peoples of the world" that stressed the need for states to support the spread of information and communication technologies (ICT) in a way that promoted economic growth, respect for human rights, and youth empowerment.

Why would the UN General Assembly select Tunisia to hold a landmark summit on freedom and the information society when its government was notorious for persecuting young internet users? The most conceivable answer is that Tunisia was being rewarded for being a beacon of secularism in the Muslim world, and for serving as a model of market liberalization in the region. The Tunisian regime complied with the aggressive structural adjustment and privatization polices dictated by global finance institutions. More to the point, it did so by selling off state resources to a small inner circle of family members and allies of the president and first lady. Ben Ali's own family held a monopoly on all business related to the internet. The government's vigorous enforcement of austerity measures, including the removal of food subsidies and dismantling of welfare state support, coupled with the summary violations of civil and human rights, would eventually push the society to revolt.

In 2006, the year after hosting the historic information summit, Tunisia's internet agency, known mockingly among activists as "Ammar404" (404 being the code for "page not found"), built a daunting firewall and used software to hack sites with Tunisian political content. In 2007 it blocked YouTube, and in 2008 it temporarily blocked Facebook. In 2009, Freedom House described Tunisia as "among the most aggressive governments in policing the internet."[8] In 2010, the Committee to Protect Journalists (CPJ) listed Tunisia as one of the ten most dangerous places to be a blogger. The country ranked a dismal 164 out of 178 in the 2010 Press Freedom Index. (Egypt ranked 127.)

Despite the many attempts by the government to censor and restrict online spaces, Facebook effectively served as "revolution headquarters" during Tunisia's twenty-nine-day revolt that led to Ben Ali's downfall. During the Tunisian uprising, Facebook membership soared. In October 2009, some 800,000 Tunisians were registered Facebook users. By the time Ben Ali fled the country on January 14, 2011, the number skyrocketed to 1.97 million, nearly a fifth of the population.[9] Tunisians were not simply joining Facebook, but were becoming more active users and participants on the site. A study by Samir Garbaya published in the *North African Journal*[10] showed that in the three-month period from November 2010 to January 2011, there was a considerable change in the average time Tunisians took to react to a Facebook posting. In November 2010, the response time was four days. On December 18, the day after the self-immolation of Mohamed Bouazizi, the time shortened to eight hours. By January 1, 2011, as the uprising heated up, the response time was two hours. On January 14, the day Ben Ali fled the country, the response time was a mere three minutes.

The more Facebook served as revolution headquarters and the more citizens used YouTube, Twitter, Yahoo, and Google to circulate news, coordinate their movements, spread anti-regime messages, and express their opinions, the more the Tunisian government treated the internet as enemy territory. It deleted activists' accounts and organized hacking operations to steal user passwords via phishing on Facebook, Gmail, Yahoo, and Hotmail.

Activists contacted Facebook directly, and its security team in California devised a way to protect Tunisians' accounts. For a

January 2011 article in the *Atlantic* entitled "The Inside Story of how Facebook Responded to Tunisian Hacks," Alexis Madrigal talked to Facebook's security officer, Joe Sullivan. Sullivan was extremely cautious in how he explained his team's handling of Tunisia, framing it as more of a technical rather than a political intervention: "At its core, from our standpoint, it's a security issue around passwords and making sure that we protect the integrity of passwords and accounts … It was very much a black and white security issue and less of a political issue."

However much the Facebook security team tried to depoliticize its intervention, the fact of the matter is that by the time the Tunisian uprising erupted, the US State Department had formed close ties with major high-tech corporations as part of its twenty-first-century statecraft. As reported in the *Washington Post* article "Tech Firms Hiring White House Staffers," the Obama administration "brought Facebook and Twitter to politics."[11] In addition to the State Department's 2.0 diplomacy initiatives, some of which targeted Tunisian and Egyptian internet activists, the Department of Defense and US intelligence agencies also liaised with tech companies on matters pertaining to national security. Technology companies had become deeply enmeshed in American power.

Tunisia's cyberwars escalated to even greater heights when Anonymous, the decentralized internet group that promotes online freedom, launched Operation Tunisia. During the Tunisian uprising, WikiLeaks founder Julian Assange released a series of incriminating cables detailing embezzlement and nepotism by the Ben Ali oligarchy, information that further fueled the revolt. When the government tried to block access to the cables, Operation Tunisia used the Twitter hashtag #OpTunisia to inform Tunisians about backdoor ways to access the WikiLeaks cables and protect themselves online. Anonymous also managed to hack and take down high-profile Tunisian governmental websites, including those of the stock exchange, the government Internet Agency, the Office of the President and Prime Minister, the Ministry of

Industry, and the Ministry of Foreign Affairs. These sites eventually came back online, but the attack made it clear that the Tunisian uprising was taking place on the twin battlefields of cyberspace and the streets, an intimation of things to come in Egypt.

Debating Martyrdom on the Eve of Revolution

The Khaled Said youth were watching and learning from Tunisia, and many saw glaring parallels between the two countries. Both Tunisia and Egypt had their own dictators, intolerable police states, and young male martyrs whose deaths roused people to action. The icon of Mohamed Bouazizi, however, did not appeal to some Egyptians, who found an ethical conflict in his act of suicide. When news spread that apparent copycat self-immolation suicides were taking place in Egypt—by an elderly man from Cairo, a desperately poor mother who committed the act in front of her children, and two unemployed men—a moral panic ensued. The two idioms of martyrdom and suicide were getting conflated in ways that proved troubling and complicated, and that brought ethics to the surface of the Khaled Said page.

A member of the 6th of April Movement, twenty-six-year-old Asmaa Mahfouz, came forward to ease concerns about suicide/martyrdom and to rally people to take to the streets on January 25. Her vlog (video blog), posted on the Khaled Said page, went viral on January 18, 2011. She categorically refused to stigmatize Egyptian self-immolators and instead held the corrupt politicians and unfair system accountable for their deaths. She turned these people who committed suicide into courageous martyrs and framed them as participants in a freedom struggle:

Four Egyptians have set themselves on fire to protest humiliation and hunger and poverty and the degradation they had to live with for thirty years. Four Egyptians have set themselves on fire, thinking maybe we can have a revolution like Tunisia … maybe we can have freedom, justice, honor, and human dignity. Today, one of these four has died. I heard people commenting: "may God forgive him, he committed a sin and killed himself for nothing" ... These self-immolators were not afraid of death, but we are afraid of the security forces ... I will not set myself on fire! If the security forces want to set me on fire let them come and do it! ... If you have honor and dignity as a man, come. Come and protect me and other girls in the protest ... Don't be afraid of the government. Fear none but God! God says that He "will not change the condition of a people until they change what is in themselves" (Quran 13:11).

Mahfouz links issues of suicide to freedom struggles, to courage to take to the streets, to manhood, and finally to Islam. When the admin posted the link to her video, he reinforced the gendered message by writing: "Esmaa Mahfouz ... a girl who is more manly than 100 men ... thank you Esmaa ... you have to listen to her."

As plans got underway for the January 25 protest, the trope of martyrdom moved more prominently into the foreground. The admin wrote, "I'm willing to die for my country, be a martyr (*shaheed*)." In another emotional post, a KS youth named Khaled Mansour declared:

I'm going down on the 25th in the first truly peaceful Egyptian Revolution. I'm ready to die. I know freedom does not come for free. And just as there were martyrs in Tunisia, I'm ready to be the first martyr for the freedom of Egypt, for its dignity. So pray for me, and may God make me succeed.

The Khaled Said youth continued to raise ethical questions about Bouazizi and suicide. The admin struggled to find a way to acknowledge the revolutionary value of Bouazizi, while also condemning his suicide, which goes against the precepts of Islam. The admin wrote:

Suicide is forbidden (*haram*). Suicide is loss of hope. Suicide is despairing of God's mercy. People commit suicide because they feel the oppression, they feel the poverty, they feel the corruption. They have the feeling they are no longer human beings, and have no value or dignity. We have to really unite with one another and become one hand so that we can stop this travesty. You, government, with all your [so-called] achievements, ENOUGH! The people are killing themselves and they're dying infidels (*kafara*) because of you.

Members on the page persisted with the suicide debate. Some people took the position that suicide was not necessarily a sin and could even be considered a heroic act when done as part of a freedom struggle, while others squarely condemned it on the grounds that a Muslim who commits suicide dies an infidel and therefore cannot reach heaven. The admin tried to settle the debates by declaring:

Committing suicide is wrong ... There is no sane human being who would support it. But to all the people who say that the one who commits suicide is an infidel, that's wrong. Committing suicide is a huge sin in the book of sins in Islam. The punishment for suicide is harsher than that for murder. But [the act of suicide] does not expel a person from his religious community (*milla*). On the Day of Judgment, the punishment for the person who committed suicide is eternity in hell unless God, may He be glorified, decides to be merciful. It's allowed for Muslims to pray for mercy and forgiveness for the person who commits suicide.

The issue was not put to rest so easily. One young man commented:

That's it, I have to speak up. Anyone who dies through suicide dies an infidel (*kafir*). Please, don't get into the whirlpool of religion so that things don't get confused. Religious fatwas have specialized people to make them. Not just anyone can say anything. *Committing suicide is wrong and has become a phenomenon.*

The admin posted a link to an Islamic website, Islamqa.com, that had a fatwa (a non-binding opinion of an Islamic scholar) on the topic of suicide. He implored the group: "Look at the link. This is a [legitimate] religious fatwa. [I challenge] you to find one fatwa that says that committing suicide makes someone an infidel. Stop making judgments on who is an infidel because judging a person as an infidel is a crime."

The debate around suicide and martyrdom became an opportunity for genuine reflection and soul-searching by the community. The KS youth asked themselves and each other: Are we ethical? Do we have values? What are our values? What is our understanding of what is ethical, moral, and just? These questions were neither scripted nor imposed from professional marketers or outside interests. As the community deliberated about their core values, this youthful society refused dogma and began the process of constructing a foundation for the future. Their exercise in group introspection was cut short, however, when the admin, in a hurry to make plans for a successful mobilization on January 25, put an end to the debate with a pithy slogan: "No to committing suicide, yes to rights." With this marketing catchphrase, he shut the door on deliberation and moved the group back to political campaign mode.

The Poverty Imperative

The Khaled Said admins joined a larger coalition of human rights activists, colleagues from the 6th of April Youth Movement, and members from the Muslim Brotherhood to make preparations for January 25. Tunisian activists also lent helpful advice about ways to reach people offline and how to set up street barricades, protect oneself from tear gas and rubber bullets, and prepare for a probable government shutdown of communications networks.

Egyptian activists working through the "We Are All Khaled Said" page understood that to carry out an effective mass mobilization required broadening the scope of the Khaled Said campaign to encompass more than anti-Emergency Law and anti-torture activities. They needed to talk about poverty, high food prices (which drew many to the streets in Tunisia), and unemployment, the scourge of the region. The page attempted to give a crash course on poverty and the economy. On January 16, 2011, the admin reported that 40 percent of Egyptians lived under the poverty line, a figure the admin would repeat several times. The anti-poverty campaign kicked off with this post:

On the 25th of January … we will ask for our rights. We want to focus from now until the 25th on the country's economic situation, about our financial situation, our daily life. We want to communicate with the ordinary poor man on the street whose main concern is where he's going to get his next piece of bread, gas for his stove, and the connection for his TV. Let's not talk about big ideas so that we find only 1000 or 2000 people in the streets. The Tunisian youth started by demanding solutions to unemployment and rising [food] prices. And when the government did not respond, they moved. We have to do the same.

At this juncture, AbdelRahman Mansour was called to begin his compulsory military service. From January 17, 2011 he was cut off from all communication and the page lost its distinctive voice. A coalition of activists continued the page's new poverty message, but fumbled as they tried to recalibrate the page's core message.

In an attempt to convince everyone to take to the streets on January 25, the admin cited the combined causes of poverty, hunger, poor-quality education, and rights. As the page tried to incorporate a wider scope of social, economic, and political problems, it lost its footing. The messaging became somewhat incoherent and muddled. A January 20 post read:

> Go down so that it doesn't remain a chaos! People are eating from the trash! The percentage of poverty in Egypt reached 40 percent. The education has been ruined and students aren't learning anything except oppression and memorization. Go down so that the Ministry of Interior doesn't violate the dignity of Egyptians. Go down so that your brother doesn't get killed. Go down so we can fix our country because unfortunately it's a mess now.

The phrase "eating from the trash" appeared in several posts. Egypt's Facebook youth likely adopted this phrase and image from the riveting song "Mr. President" by the Tunisian rapper El General (whose real name is Hamada Ben Aoun). This low-budget recording was posted on YouTube and went viral in Tunisia and around the Arab world at the start of the Tunisian uprising. In the emotionally raw video, El General sings:

> There are still people dying of hunger who want to work to survive, but their voice is not heard … People have become like animals see the police with batons, takatak … This is a message from one of your children who is telling of his suffering. We are living like dogs. Half of the people are living in filth and drink from a cup of suffering. Mr. President your people are dead. Many people eat from the trash. You see what is happening in the country, misery everywhere and people who have not found a place to sleep … Mr. President … I decided to send this message even though the people told me that my end is death.

After the song's release El General was arrested, but later set free.

After repeating the message that people are eating from the trash, the admin called on members to send pictures that document poverty and unemployment. He tried to transfer the techniques of an anti-torture campaign to an anti-poverty campaign. Many people sent in photos of street children with ragged clothes and soiled faces. Images of poor children, however, do not translate into easy solutions or clearly defined demands. The activists were not able to come up with a convincing set of targets to address the blight of poverty.

Pressed for time, and without ideas about how to deal in any meaningful way with poverty and inequality, a coalition of activists and opposition political figures drafted a statement to outline the goals of the revolution. The document, "Everything You Want to Know About the Revolution of January 25," was accessible through the KS page. It spelled out four demands pertaining to poverty, the Emergency Law, the Interior Minister, and presidential terms:

Document about goals of January 25
    What are our demands?
    There are 4 demands
    1. Confronting the problem of poverty before it explodes by complying with the Egyptian law to increase the minimum wage, especially for people working in the health and education sectors so that we can improve public services. Unemployment benefits of at least 500 pounds should be offered to any recent college graduate without work for a limited period.
    2. Cancelling the Emergency Law which allows State Security to control Egypt. The law allows members of the political opposition to be put in prison without due process. We demand that police stations stop organized torture. We demand that the Egyptian government respects court verdicts.
    3. To get rid of Interior Minister Habib al-Adly, due to the security chaos that Egypt has been facing. Members of the Ministry of Interior act with impunity as they carry out terrorist acts and an abundance of crimes.
    4. To put a limit on presidential terms to two consecutive terms.

Absolute power leads to corruption. There is no developed country that allows its president to stay in power for tens of years. It's our right to choose our president and to ensure that no one uses his power to oppress and rule the country until he dies.

Egyptians have several other demands, like improving health and education. But as a start we should all move together to achieve one demand at a time by putting pressure on the government. As the people, our role is to direct the government, hold them accountable, evaluate their performance, and define the priorities, not vice versa.

In the document, poverty is reduced to two demands: raising the minimum wage, and providing unemployment benefits to university graduates for a limited period. These goals come across as ad hoc when compared to the more pointed demands of eliminating the Emergency Law, removing Interior Minister Habib al-Adly from office, and limiting presidential terms. The campaigners proved incapable of formulating ideas about how to achieve an alternative economic order and address the structural causes of poverty and skewed wealth distribution. They were, however, able to coin a catchy slogan that would gain national traction and come to represent the demands of the people: "Bread, Freedom, Social Justice" (*aysh, hurriya, idala ijtimaiyya*).

On the afternoon of January 25, 2011, a date set from a Facebook page, the most momentous uprising in Egypt in over half a century began. The organizers of the revolutionary event could hardly have imagined that within hours, the numbers of people in the streets of Cairo, Alexandria, Suez, Ismailia, and Mansoura would swell so rapidly. People from all walks of life, across generations, social classes, genders, and professional groups, would join the cause initiated by the Facebook youth. By the night of January 25, the wheels of revolt were in motion.

CHAPTER SIX

Memes and the War of Ideas

On January 25, 2011, Egypt's youth of the internet made history as the first group to trigger a mass uprising from a Facebook page. On Thursday, January 27, the Mubarak regime made history as the first government to impose a five-day shutdown of all mobile and digital communications. By the time the government pulled the communications plug, the uprising was unstoppable. There was no off switch that could deactivate this wired generation, which had coalesced, at least momentarily, as a counter-power. News outlets reported widely about how the Facebook youth had used social media to set the date for an uprising and prepare for the mobilization. They expressed amazement at how the crowds swelled as the youth of the internet marched through the streets and called on their fellow citizens to join them, entreating them with chants like "Bread, Freedom, Social Justice" (*aysh, hurriya, idala ijtimaiyya)*, and "The People Want to Bring Down the Regime" (*as-shaab yurid iskat il-nizam*), a chant which traveled around the Arab world from Tunisia. When the internet returned on February 2, the world's gaze was on Tahrir Square, the symbolic heart of the revolution. The square provided the political stage for the people's uprising. Yet a struggle just as consequential was taking place out of sight, in the virtual corridors and alleyways of Facebook. The site turned into a battleground where a war of ideas was being fought, sometimes to the death. Rival sides battled over ideas as consequential as the nature of freedom, the shape of democracy, and the preparedness of Egyptians to bring forth a more radical and participatory order. We can glean the tenor and evolution of Egypt's culture wars through an investigation of Facebook from 2011 to 2013.

In his seminal work *The Selfish Gene*, Richard Dawkins tries to unveil the mechanisms through which culture spreads. Drawing on the metaphor of biology, he has famously written: "Just as genes propagate themselves in the gene pool by leaping from body to body via sperms or eggs, so memes propagate themselves in the meme pool by leaping from brain to brain via a process which, in the broad sense, can be called imitation." Memes, in their most basic form, are what Dawkins calls "units of cultural transmission."[1] According to *Merriam-Webster's Dictionary*, a meme can be "an idea, behavior, style, or usage that spreads from person to person within a culture." Dawkins implies that memes lack intentionality. His theory gives little credence to how people actively produce memes in an attempt to disrupt, reinforce, or otherwise intervene into culture. Sometime memes go viral spontaneously, but memes also enter the consciousness and bounce from mind to mind through a manipulated and deliberate process. Dawkins's indifference to human agency, marketing, and hierarchies of power is not a mere theoretical shortcoming. A biologically inspired theory of culture renders the study of culture the objective domain of science, outside of politics, the market, human struggle, and the realm of ideology.

One of the most powerful mechanisms through which ideology functions is the invisibility mechanism. People cannot reflect on, struggle against, and change what they do not see. What we aim to show by looking at memes is that memes have consequences in the war of position. They are produced and circulated by social actors with interests, stakes, and clear relations—be they antagonistic or in allegiance—to power. Given the hidden nature of ideology, meme makers sometimes think they are working against the interests of the system, when in fact they may be supporting and reproducing it.

Virtual spaces are multilayered and dynamic. They incorporate myriad actors with overlapping and shifting interests. In the memetic war, it is not always possible to pigeonhole a person or group to a particular position. There are, for instance, the corporations that try to monetize and manipulate user behavior, tech engineers who are driven by the desire to innovate, security forces that track and monitor users, and anti- and pro-system hackers and spies who go to great lengths to advance their own causes. Notwithstanding the importance of all these forces, we will isolate and focus on two groups in the virtual wars: the "virtual warriors," Egyptian revolutionaries who try to keep alive the culture of dissent as they work to pave the way for a New Order, and the counterrevolutionary forces that use Facebook to rein in and thwart opposing voices.

Opposing sides in the virtual war create and spread memes, which we will call "vemes" (virtual memes). Following on Dawkins's biological metaphor, vemes are ideas whose conception, birth, and proliferation occur inside virtual spaces. Social media is a giant veme machine where vemes spread and evolve like a fast-growing organism. A distinct characteristic of the veme is the speed at which it moves and mutates, the volume of people and spaces it has the potential to encounter as it circulates, and the rapidity with which it expires. Adversarial vemes are constantly at war with each other. As the vemetic war escalates, the vemes become more extreme and radical.

To illustrate how vemetic wars have played out in relation to the Egyptian uprising, we will isolate five phases over a three-year period. Phase 1 involves a clash between the vemes of the Mubarak state and the professional cyberactivist veme-makers. During Phase 2, the Muslim Brotherhood, with an already deep and wide presence in social media, unleashed its e-militias (electronic militias) to try to conquer the space and build its own virtual empire.

Phase 3 saw an evolutionary leap in the agility of the revolutionary veme-makers, whose vemes overtook the Brotherhood vemes. Phase 4 turned into an actual militarized war on the streets against the admins of revolutionary Facebook pages, who paid for their vemes with their lives. Phase 5 ushered in a second revolution and counter-revolution.

Phase 1: The Demise of Pre-Digital Power

On February 2, 2011, Egyptian Facebookers logged back into the site after a five-day hiatus. They encountered a fluttering of pro-Mubarak vemes positioned strategically throughout Egyptian Facebook spaces. The images of Mubarak, static and humorless, had the uncanny feel of Iron Curtain–style propaganda posters. The purpose of these vemes was to trick Facebookers into thinking that January 25 was actually a day of loyalty to the president, not a day of revolt. One pro-Mubarak veme displayed the president buttoned up in a suit wearing sunglasses. It read: "January 25, 2011, Day of Allegiance to the Leader and Commander. We are all with you and our hearts are with you. The campaign for Mubarak. Security for Egypt." Another veme depicted a smiling Mubarak superimposed over the Egyptian flag with the words, "With all my heart I love you Egypt, and I love you oh President."

Mubarak e-militias spread pro-regime vemes, but their creators did not seem to grasp the differences between traditional media and new media in terms of style, production, and circulation. In media of the pre-digital age (radio, print, and television), messages are professionally produced and disseminated in a top-down direction. Their success depends on accessing a receiving audience. Social media, in contrast, works in a more horizontal and crowdsourced way. For a veme to be really effective, it must spread through the volition of scores of networked people. Online marketers and astute virtual creators understand how to design vemes to get them into circulation and maximize their impact. The Mubarak e-militias had no such aptitude. They approached social media with a vertical, as opposed to a horizontal, understanding.

The Mubarak e-militias tried to infiltrate the opposition spaces on Facebook, but with little success, since their fake profiles were easy to recognize. They also used social media as a means to support the president, his heir, and his National Democratic Party. Prior to January 25, the Mubarak e-militias tried to direct people to the Facebook fan page of Gamal Mubarak, the president's son who was being groomed for the presidency.

During Phase 1, the Mubarak e-militias competed and battled mainly against professionally trained veme-makers, such as those from the pages of "We Are All Khaled Said" and the 6th of April Movement. An especially popular veme from these pages was inspired by the Obama 2008 presidential campaign. In this veme, the words "Yes We Can" are superimposed over a young man's face painted with the Egyptian flag. The man's face, with his green eyes and foreign features, appears more European than North African, which raises questions about whether this was an organic homegrown veme, or an externally produced one with the goal of reinforcing Western ideas of power, beauty, and politics. The youthful, pro-revolution vemes that circulated prior to and during the eighteen-day uprising exuded youth lifestyles, often in the style of advertising.

The Mubarak government's misunderstanding of new media spaces signaled that it was losing control over a part of its ideological apparatus. It did not understand how mechanisms of persuasion function in the virtual age. The more the Mubarak regime lost the virtual war during the January 25 revolt, the more it resorted to sheer force to subdue the population. Each new wave of killings during the eighteen-day protest, producing new lists of martyrs, fueled the protests further, both online and in the streets. On February 11, 2011, with pressure from the people and, supposedly, orders from the military, Mubarak surrendered.

After the fall of Mubarak on February 11, the interim military government, the Supreme Council of Armed Forces (SCAF), aggressively digitized. It established a Facebook page and a Twitter feed to post communiqués to citizens. Within days, the SCAF Facebook page garnered over one million "Likes." Similar to the Mubarak government, SCAF continued to use social media in a top-down manner that did not sufficiently factor in the horizontal architecture of the space.

In summary, during Phase 1 the Mubarak and SCAF e-militias were weak because they entered social media spaces with a pre-digital approach. They tried to conquer the space by asserting a formal presence over it, rather than interacting with it in a crowdsourced and networked way. During this phase the revolutionaries were at an advantage, either because they received formal training in cyberactivism, or because they grew up in virtual environments and had an intuitive understanding of how to master these spaces.

Phase 2: E-Militias of the Muslim Brotherhood

During Egypt's first-ever presidential runoff in June 2012, Facebook pages were ablaze with political commentary. The runoff was between Muslim Brotherhood candidate Mohamed Morsi and former Mubarak-era Prime Minister Ahmed Shafik. A veme that circulated widely on Facebook at that time depicted Hassan al-Banna, the founder of the Muslim Brotherhood, with the words, "By the way, I'm not from the Brotherhood. I disagree with them on a lot of issues but I respect them." The quote is signed "Hassan al-Banna." The veme used satire to hint at a truth that many social media users had been suspecting, even if they lacked hard proof—namely, that the Muslim Brotherhood had been infiltrating social media in ways that were far from transparent. Vemes such as this served as a counter-mechanism to alert social media users to tread more cautiously and critically on Facebook, to not fall victim to the indoctrination machinery of groups whose aim was to co-opt the revolution.

Since its founding in Ismailia in 1928, the Muslim Brotherhood (MB) has prioritized working in institutions that deal with the ideological and cultural conditioning of children and youth. The schoolteacher Hassan al-Banna understood very well the principle that whomever captures the youth captures the nation. Even as the Brotherhood operated as an outlawed and persecuted organization through most of its existence, it managed to maintain an especially robust presence in Egyptian schools, in teacher-training units at colleges of education, in student unions at universities, and in after-school and summer sports clubs. All these sites served as key recruiting grounds to grow the movement. Starting in the 1990s the Brotherhood capitalized on the liberalization of media and communications to spread its anti-regime and pan-Islamic ideology through satellite television and the internet.

In the lead-up to Egypt's parliamentary elections in October 2010, Brotherhood members anonymously established the Facebook page "Network of the Martyr" (*Shabakat al-Shahid*). This page reported on the 2010 parliamentary elections with an eye to documenting electoral fraud and police abuse. After a successful test run, it was relaunched as "Rasd," meaning, "monitor." As related by Rehab Sakr in her research about the Muslim Brotherhood's online networks, the Rasd admins identified themselves only as "Egyptian youth who have a desire to present the real practices of the regime during the elections through an alternative media channel since the official media is completely dominated by the political regime." They made it appear as if Rasd was an entirely nonpartisan site, "a media created by the audience." The admins made no mention of their affiliation with the Brotherhood. The page called on all its Facebook fans to monitor the elections in their districts and to send pictures and videos documenting election irregularities for its virtual wall.[2]

In *Revolution 2.0*, Wael Ghonim claims that in December

2010, after the fall of Tunisian dictator Ben Ali, he personally advised one of the Rasd admins, Amr El-Qazzaz, an active Muslim Brotherhood member, to open a new Rasd page entirely devoted to the January 25 Revolution. With the help of the Khaled Said page and other pages, the new page gained over one million subscribers in a matter of days. Ghonim writes about the Rasd page as "neutral," and "a source of information and not a source of analysis or bias."[3] Nonetheless, the page's pro-Muslim Brotherhood bias became evident during the presidential campaign, and its mask came off entirely as Rasd grew into a regional platform—with branches in Libya, Syria, Morocco, Turkey, and Palestine—to report on Arab uprisings from a pro-Muslim Brotherhood perspective.

The Brotherhood worked literally around the clock to influence public opinion, both through its twenty-four-hour television channel, Al Jazeera Mubasher Misr, and by mobilizing its e-militias to spread its message online. Brotherhood members and supporters acted as the group's virtual foot soldiers. They spread pro-Brotherhood vemes deep within the arteries of social media. The Brotherhood leadership distributed a document, "Accusations and Answers" (*Shobohat wa Rudud*), to provide members with talking points about how to address critics of Morsi and the MB in social media spaces. The e-militias prefaced their talking points with phrases like, "I'm not Muslim Brotherhood but I respect them," "I hate the Muslim Brotherhood but I have to support Morsi to get rid of Shafik," "I know they're looking out for their own interests but they were my companions in Tahrir square," "Don't let your hate for the MB blind you," "The MB are selfish but they're not criminal," and so on.

The more the e-militias spread their scripted talking points, the more they exposed themselves and their strategies on social media. In one instance, two separate people posted identical comments to the discussion board of a popular anti-Brotherhood Facebook page called "I Dreamed of the Square Before the [Brotherhood's]

Millions Occupied It" (*Halimt bil-Midan Qabla an Yaskunu al Milyaeen*). A certain Tamer Fouad and a certain Ashraf Abed, each from his own separate profile, wrote the following:

> To put it briefly, to those of you who are thinking about making a revolution against the Brotherhood, the election was very fair and free from any rigging. The majority of Egyptians elected Morsi. So let's give him a chance and see how he'll do. You were silent for thirty years, so why can't you be patient for just one year before [complaining]. By the way, I swear to God that I'm not from the Brotherhood. I just speak the truth.

The page's admin created a veme showing the two identical comments and spread it around, calling the two posters the Muslim Brotherhood's "copy and paste committee."

The MB e-militias used numerous other techniques in addition to the copy and paste strategy to try to colonize social media spaces. We outline a sampling of their techniques below.

DENYING AND DISGUISING

During the 2012 presidential campaign, it came to light that numerous pages that initially appeared to be independent youth-run pages were orchestrated platforms with complete loyalty to the Brotherhood. The admins of these pages first denied that they were involved with the Brotherhood, and then used all their sway to support and defend the group. In a common style of denial, an admin insisted he could not possibly be aligned with the Brotherhood because he smoked, didn't pray much at the mosque, and wore jeans. One such page, "The Square is the Solution" (*Al-Midan Huwa al-Hal*), was inundated with accusations that it was a Brotherhood page because of its relentless campaigning for Morsi. The admin, in his defense, wrote in July 2012:

Do I need to constantly say that I'm not from the Muslim
Brotherhood and that this is not a Brotherhood page
   I swear I smoke cigarettes, two packs per day
   I don't even pray in the mosque except for the Friday prayer
   And I wear jeans :)
   Enough!!!!!!!!

RIDICULING THE OPPOSITION

The Brotherhood's e-militias worked hard to circulate vemes to
ridicule and discredit the political opposition. One Facebook page
was solely devoted to discrediting Hamdeen Sabahi, the popular
Nasserite candidate who came very close to making the presidential runoff. The page was called "Hamdeen Sabahi is Someone
Who Fooled Us" (*Hamdeen Sabahi Wahid Khamena*). The title is a
play on the words of Sabahi's campaign slogan, "Hamdeen Sabahi
is One of Us" (*Hamdeen Sabahi Wahid Minina*).

These vemes lacked subtlety and humor, and served more
as crass smear propaganda. For instance, one veme depicted
Hamdeen Sabahi as a devil with horns, and below the image was
the caption "Sabahi, the Man Against Islam and For Corruption."
Another used the image of Gandhi to discredit the two most
popular and important members of the opposition, Hamdeen
Sabahi and Mohamed ElBaradei. Next to an image of Gandhi,
the text read: "The two who we can't trust: Hamdeen Sabahi
and the Twitter Man." It was signed "Gandhi." The term "Twitter
Man" was used by ElBaradei's adversaries to undermine his effective and wide-ranging social media campaign that combined
tweets, a Facebook page, and direct messaging to people via
YouTube videos.

Another veme showed Sabahi with an inane expression surrounded by a childish scene with colorful balloons, conveying
the message that he was foolish and unfit for adult responsibili-
ties. These vemes were not intended to generate debate or raise

awareness about actual flaws of the targeted candidates. Their sole purpose was to make the political opposition appear inept and unqualified for the presidency. These vemes lacked the creativity, wit, and craftiness of homegrown youthful vemes.

APPROPRIATING THE LANGUAGE OF REVOLUTION

In his book *Whose Freedom?*, the linguist and cognitive scientist George Lakoff argues that "repetition of language has the power to change brains." In his research on the rise of the conservative right in the US, he shows that "the word 'freedom,' if repeatedly associated with radical conservative themes, may be learned not with its traditional progressive meaning, but with a radical conservative meaning. 'Freedom' is being redefined brain by brain."[4] The MB e-militia pages tried to appropriate and redefine the political vocabulary of the revolution to confuse and manipulate people's cognitive frames. The e-militias took words with symbolic power, like "democracy," "old regime" (*felool*), and "revolution," and attempted to strip them of any emancipatory meaning, recalibrating them to mean an unquestioning and uncritical support of Muslim Brotherhood rule.

The word "*felool*," which refers to the corrupt remnants of the old regime and their supporters, was recast to mean anyone who dared to criticize the Muslim Brotherhood. The anti-*felool* page "Two Felools and One Tameyya" (*Etnen Felool wa Wahid Taamia*) was launched in July 2011. The name of the page is a play on the words "*felool*" and "*foul*," the name of the famous Egyptian bean dish. The page gained a large following as a supposed independent anti-Mubarak page. It later attempted to change the meaning of *felool* from a supporter of the old regime to "people who support the army, police, judiciary, security, and anyone who doesn't support the Muslim Brotherhood." By this definition, anyone not in favor of the Brotherhood was cast as a traitor to the revolution.

GLORIFYING THE DESPOT

In November 2012, President Mohamed Morsi granted himself unprecedented and sweeping powers that exceeded those held even by Hosni Mubarak. He appointed Muslim Brotherhood figures to key government posts, regardless of their qualifications. As anti-Muslim Brotherhood sentiments escalated in the country, the MB's e-militias went into overdrive. They spread pro-Morsi vemes and opened numerous Facebook accounts to convey the message that Morsi was a fair and seasoned statesman and the pillar of nationalism. Images circulated of Morsi standing erect in a well-tailored suit surrounded by the regalia of the state—the flag and national stamp with the eagle. The pro-Morsi vemes had a striking similarity to Mubarak-era presidential portraits.

DEMONIZING FACEBOOK

When the Brotherhood was a political opposition group, the MB e-militias held dominion over a large territory of the Egyptian part of Facebook. When the Brotherhood took state power, they lost their advantage in the realm of social media, which remained a space of dissent that was difficult to control. Much of the youthful anti-Mubarak energy transferred to anti-Brotherhood energy, since the same problems of repression, autocracy, patriarchy, and corruption persisted under Brotherhood rule. As they lost ground, Brotherhood leaders tried to discredit the online space. The popular Muslim Brotherhood television preacher Safwat Hegazy compared Facebook and Twitter to Allata and Aluzza, the pagan statues that stood at the Kaaba in Mecca during the time of the Prophet Mohammed. In July 2012, he proclaimed in a televised broadcast that "Facebook and Twitter are the False Prophet" (*mosaylama el-kazzab*), meaning they were deceiving people and should be shunned. At the same time, the Brotherhood elders made a strong push for Egyptian youth to join their own social media alternatives: Ikhwan Twitter, Ikhwantube, Ikhwanwiki, and

Ikhwanbook. These sites resembled the popular sites they imitated—namely Twitter, YouTube, WikiLeaks, and Facebook—with the notable exception that they did not allow users autonomy, did not allow for crowdsourcing, and operated with a high degree of control and censorship. Needless to say, these Brotherhood services did not draw large numbers of users away from the platforms they imitated.

In Phase 2, the MB e-militias set out to conquer social media, and for some time they held an advantage. However, as the tactics of the e-militias were discovered, and as the reputation of the MB in the wider society plummeted, the e-militias lost their edge in cyberspace. The cyber-battles would continue into Phase 3.

Phase 3: Virtual Warriors Gain the Advantage

Phase 3 marked the rise of grassroots, homegrown virtual warriors and the retreat of NGO-trained e-militias and the Muslim Brotherhood e-militias. The culture war reached new heights as the agile virtual revolutionaries metaphorically attacked and destroyed society's icons through satire, language, and images. Nothing was sacred for these young veme-makers, who battled hypocrisy and vice in the search for a new truth.

A widespread complaint among Egyptians in the post-Mubarak period was that the Islamist-dominated parliament and presidency spent far more energy on trying to curb cultural freedoms than on addressing economic and infrastructural problems. The new government carried on endless debates about women's clothing, alcohol, bathing suits, relations between the sexes, and women's roles, all topics which further marginalized women and non-Muslim minorities. It is no wonder that Phase 3 was fueled by a disdain for religious institutions and icons.

A new Facebook page calling itself "The Committee for the Promotion of Cabbage and Prevention of Hamburger in Egypt" (*hi`at al-amr bil malfoof aan al-hamburger fil Masr*) was created.

This title was a play on the name of the infamous morality police in Saudi Arabia, the Committee for the Promotion of Virtue and the Prevention of Vice (*hi`at al-amr bil-ma`aruf wa al-nahi aan al-mankar*). The page claimed that its purpose was not to insult the Quran or Islam, but to criticize the Islamist political forces that were promoting a superficial understanding of democracy and using their power to try to make everything in the culture forbidden (*haram*).

The page's signature veme (Figure 6.1) showed the face of a famous Islamist preacher, Mohamed Hussein Yaqoub, proclaiming a "yes" vote for the hamburger. The veme was a wink to the elections of March 2011, when Islamist candidates won the majority vote. Yaqoub declared at the time, "The election boxes said yes to religion." This meme drew attention to the shallow way Islamists were selling religion to the Egyptian public, as if could be advertised in the style of a fast food ad.

The page reminded youth that they had been rebelling against the state for many years and knew how to outsmart the system. One veme showed students expertly climbing over different types of school walls with the caption: "Mohamed Morsi raises the walls around his castle. Does he really think this is an effective way [to stop] a generation whose favorite pastime was jumping over school walls?" This veme sent the message that in the absence of legitimate and fair authority, the enterprising younger generation would continue to find ways to escape the system and learn and live freely outside of it.

Another meme depicts the Muslim Brotherhood leaders Mohamed Morsi and Khairat al-Shater as Egypt's mafia, akin to the Corleone family from *The Godfather*.

A satirical page of a different nature, "Falota Fans," used pop art and advertising vemes to speak truth to power while having a bit of fun. It directed satire even against itself by using the colloquial word "*falota*"—someone who falsely claims to be an expert—in its name. Many of its vemes were composed of four colorful

Figure 6.1: "[Vote] Yes for the Hamburger." Veme from Facebook page "The Committee for the Promotion of Cabbage and Prevention of Hamburger in Egypt," 2013

Figure 6.2: The Brotherhood. From the Facebook page "The Committee for the Promotion of Cabbage and Prevention of Hamburger in Egypt," 2013

repetitive frames in the style of Andy Warhol. One veme featured four frames depicting the Muslim Brotherhood leader and businessman Khairat al-Shater. The purpose of this veme (Figure 6.3) was to reveal the double discourse of the Muslim Brotherhood, which presented a mask of liberalism and tolerance to Western audiences, but a message of bigotry and uncompromising rule to its Arab constituents. The Arabic words "Islamic State" are translated into English as "Modern Democratic Civil State," the Arabic "I hate Christians for Allah" is translated as "I love all Christians," and "Muslims participating in non-Muslim feasts are infidels" appears in English as "Merry Christmas."

The Facebook page "Carlos Latuff," named after the Brazilian/ Lebanese cartoonist, dealt with the virtual war in a serious, shrewd, and educational way. The admin of the "Carlos Latuff" page (Carlos) saw himself as the watchdog of the revolutionary society on Facebook. Carlos displayed high levels of what we will call "virtual intelligence," meaning he possessed a mix of

Figure 6.3: Exposing political doublespeak. From "Falota Fans," 2013

intuition, internet investigative skills, and networking prowess which enabled him to uncover all manner of hidden wars and positions on social media.

Carlos became a social media sensation because of his astuteness at revealing the Muslim Brotherhood e-militias. During the Morsi presidency, the page kept a running list of Facebook pages suspected of being Muslim Brotherhood platforms. Carlos also called out liberal revolutionary pages for taking positions he viewed as counter-revolutionary. During the 2012 presidential elections, Carlos raised questions about the "We Are All Khaled Said" page, especially after Wael Ghonim publicly endorsed Mohamed Morsi for president. He referred to the page as "We Are All Hassan Al Banna," a moniker which spread. As it turned out, the Khaled Said page was not easy to pin down. Carlos changed his position on it several times. He referred to it variously as a Brotherhood page, a revolutionary page infiltrated by Muslim Brothers, and a page that had lost its way.

Carlos and Falota Fans were preoccupied with keeping the revolution alive in virtual spaces. Other pages concentrated on raising awareness about the deteriorating situation on the streets. A veme from the Facebook page "That's It, We Had a Revolution" showed a real photo of a trash-filled street with the caption "There is no image expressing what's happening in Egypt better than this." This photo was so subversive because in the frame was an official banner, rising from the mountain of trash, with the words "The project of the government to improve the level of cleanliness. Plan of the 100 days." The hundred-day plan was Morsi's big campaign promise, but it never materialized.

The Czech-born philosopher Vilém Flusser posits that the purpose of a photo is to frame a part of reality. Since the viewer understands that an image shows just a partial reality, photography cannot be a strictly political form. We argue that photography can be a political act when the purpose of a photo is to make the point that nothing is real except this frame. This veme conveys the message that the pile of trash with the government banner rising from it exemplifies the situation in the country. The photo not only frames the failure of the system, but it calls attention to the system's own lies and ineptitude. This photograph served as a strong message that the Egyptian people would not let Morsi forget that he had broken his promise to them.

Phase 4: Kill the Admin

The virtual wars escalated to especially dangerous heights in Phase 4, which witnessed the torture and killing of a number of virtual warriors. The first fatality of Phase 4 was seventeen-year-old Gika, the admin of the popular Facebook page "We Are All Against the Muslim Brotherhood."

On November 19, 2012, Gika prepared to go to Mohamed Mahmoud Street to join his comrades for the one-year anniversary of the street battles demanding justice for the families of the martyrs of the revolution. He understood the risks. The previous year, security forces had killed over forty mainly young male protesters, and shot into the eyes of scores of others, which gave rise to the street's revolutionary name, "the street of the freedom eyes." Before leaving his home, Gika posted a note on his Facebook page: "This is the last post I am writing until I return tomorrow from the street of the freedom eyes. That's if I come back." As fate would have it, he would not return home. While in the thick of the crowd, the light of a green laser landed on his body. A traitor from the 6th of April group had identified his comrade Gika for a hit man. The professional assassin shot Gika with seven bullets; one to the head, two to the chest, and four to the stomach. Gika did not stand a chance. He died of his wounds in a nearby hospital.

"Kristy" (Mohamed El-Qorany) was the next social network activist to fall. He was part of a group of admins of the popular Facebook page "The Muslim Brotherhood are Liars" (*Ikhwan Kaziboon*). Kristy participated in a demonstration in front of the presidential palace (*al-Itihadiyya*) to protest Brotherhood rule. Similarly to Gika, someone in the crowd shined a green laser on his body and soon he was shot dead, the victim of a premeditated assassination. The assault on the virtual warriors continued when "Amr Morsi" and five other admins of the page "Molotov Cola" were arrested. "Mohamed El Masry," admin of the page "Generation of Change," was kidnapped and beaten, and "Ahmed Saleh" of the page "Rights of the Martyr in Tahrir and Al Itihadiyya" was kidnapped and horrifically tortured. Female admins also suffered arrest and harassment. Nermin Hussien, admin of the page "Finally, We Had a Revolution," which posted vemes of uncollected trash to document the failure of Morsi's hundred-day plan, was arrested in February 2013.

Details surfaced about how the MB e-militias coordinated with street militias to attack activists. During the popular TV program *Cairo Today*, hosted by Amr Adib, a young woman named "Cherry," the admin of the page "The Muslim Brotherhood Has No Religion," called in and gave a riveting account of how she and her fellow admins fell prey to the machinations of the MB's e-militias. She explained that a certain "activist x" posed as someone deeply sympathetic to the cause of the page. He messaged the admins, sent them posts and news critical of the Muslim Brotherhood, and eventually gained their trust. At that point he asked if he could be listed as a fellow admin on the page so that he could post items directly, and they agreed. As a coadmin, he gained access to information about the members of the group, including details about their addresses, their networks, their correspondence, and where they met for protests. He handed over this intelligence to his superiors in the Brotherhood, who then decided how to deal with the activists on the ground.

IF YOU CAN'T CONTROL THEIR MINDS, ATTACK THEIR BODIES

Unable to control the minds and thought processes of a rebellious population, the powers that be went after their bodies. The perpetrators hailed from the security apparatus of the state, the thugs loyal to the Mubarak regime, and the Muslim Brotherhood. They attacked rebellious bodies on different fronts. A spate of coordinated gang sexual assaults took place against female protesters in Tahrir Square at about the same time the admins of Facebook pages were being kidnapped, tortured, and killed. Unlike the targeted sexual assaults on female activists during the Mubarak period, this new style of mob sexual assaults seemed more random. They were carried out to send a message to all women, not only the celebrity activists, to stay out of the square. Women responded by maintaining a robust presence in the square and by circulating testimonials, information, and memes about the assaults online and offline. An image of a graffiti painting in Tahrir Square by Mira Shihadeh and El-Zeft, entitled "The Circle of Hell," circulated widely on social media (Figure 6.4).

Figure 6.4: "The Circle of Hell." A graffiti painting by Mira Shihadeh and El-Zeft, Cairo, February 2013

THE ANTI-SYSTEM MEME MACHINE STILL WORKS

In the midst of the spate of killings, arrests, kidnappings, torture, and sexual assaults, communities of citizen-activists came together online to protect each other. One group, "Catch a Sheep," used virtual intelligence to sniff out infiltrators. The page revealed that a certain Ahmed Saeed, who posed as a liberal activist, was in fact a foot soldier for the Brotherhood's e-militia. The page traced Saeed's social media behavior back to the Mubarak era to establish this fact without a doubt. Catch a Sheep sent a threatening warning to Saeed: "We will suck your blood very soon." Scores of other people, through their personal pages, status updates, and comments on other pages, spread information about how to identify and catch masked e-militia members. A fan on the Mohamed ElBaradei page posted a warning to the community about an infiltrator:

> The secret police of the Muslim Brotherhood infiltrated the profile of Mohamed Abdullah. They are pretending that they are revolutionaries to get information about the revolutionaries and then kill them. Please everybody, we should report this guy ... share share share quickly!! We must close this guy's account to save the revolutionaries.

TAKING THE SERIOUS WAR IN A NON-SERIOUS WAY

Following Gika's murder, a question circulated online and throughout Egyptian society: "Was Gika killed because he was the admin of an anti-Brotherhood Facebook page?" By so much as asking this question, the Facebook youth showed that they underestimated their force as a counter-power and the threat they posed to the system of power.

Many young revolutionaries did not take the war against them seriously on two levels. First, they did not exhibit the psychological trauma that should manifest when your peers are being killed. In particular, the younger males seemed cavalier about death, as if they were characters and dying was part of a video game. For instance, after a rumor spread around Facebook that the admin of the page "Best Jokes" was killed in a protest, he playfully posted an image of himself holding a paper with the words "Am I dead?! J."

Second, the social media activists continued to doubt their power. They could not fathom the extent to which they presented a threat to the authorities. Even with the ongoing attacks on their fellow Facebookers, they remained surprised that the system was taking them and the virtual war so seriously. In the spring of 2013, these everyday citizen-activists felt the revolution was being revised in a serious way through the youth movement and public campaign called "Tamarud" (Rebel).

Phase 5: Nationalism Reigns

With the help of thousands of citizen volunteers, Tamarud carried out what would become the largest petition campaign and street demonstration in Egypt's history. Tamarud's two main goals were to gather millions of signatures as a vote of no confidence against Mohamed Morsi, and to call for early elections. On June 30, 2013, the group presented some seventeen million signatures to the Supreme Constitutional Court, and at least as many citizens marched through the streets around Egypt. A mere four days later, General Abdel Fattah El Sisi, responding to the "voice of the people," dissolved the Morsi government and appointed a temporary civilian government. Sitting on his televised stage of high political theater were Mohamed ElBaradei and two of the young founders of Tamarud, among others.

The fall of the Muslim Brotherhood was an enormous victory for the revolutionaries. Initially, the people called June 30 Egypt's second revolution. At the same time, a segment of the revolutionary fighters had been gearing up for a prolonged fight and their suspicions were aroused by the ease with which Morsi was unseated. Not only did they suspect the hand of the old Mubarak regime in orchestrating events from behind the scenes, but they could not believe that the military would step in to "put the revolution back on track" so swiftly. Generals are not known for harboring sympathies for people's freedom struggles.

In a matter of weeks, the people's second revolution started to smell more like a military coup. Mubarak was released from prison and Egyptian security forces carried out indiscriminate killings of Muslim Brotherhood supporters in Rabaa al-Adaweya and al-Nahda squares. Mohamed ElBaradei, who lent the interim government a high degree of credibility as the vice president, resigned after one month and returned to his other home in Austria. A post that went viral on Facebook asked: "The MB are in jail again, Mubarak is out, and ElBaradei is in Austria. Who pressed New Game?"

COUNTER-REVOLUTION TIMES?

Was this the start of the counter-revolution? Was the game really over? The military intelligence and security services seemed to have laid out an elaborate plan to conquer society by spreading memes of nationalism and loyalty to the army. On Facebook, the official page of General El Sisi was a paragon of professional social media marketing, replete with a tagline, "The Strong Man of Egypt," and an eye-catching logo—two hands forming the letter "C" with the thumb and index finger. Together, the hands spell CC, an eye catching way to show the name "Sisi."

El Sisi was presented as the patriarch of the nation, and the military was cast as the nation's unequivocal savior and protector. Any Egyptian who so much as questioned the military option was branded a traitor, a foreign spy, a supporter of the Muslim Brotherhood, and an enemy of the war on terrorism (aka, the war on the MB), or worse, someone who did not love Egypt. A post on

Figure 6.5: Cover photo from the official Facebook page of General Adbel Fatah El Sisi, "The Strong Man of Egypt," 2013

El Sisi's official page showed the silhouette of a soldier standing stoically and alone atop a hill, holding a rifle. The image was entitled "I am the military. Who are you?" (Figure 6.6):

Figure 6.6: "I'm the military. Who are you?" From the official page of Abdel Fatah El Sisi, 2013

I am the military. Who are you?
  I died for you millions of times.
  I'm in the desert eating serpents, to give you the chance to buy the luxury food you desire to eat.
  I am the one who is saving you and saving your revolution.
  And then you ask me to leave the leadership of the country?
  Who could I leave it to?
  I am the military. Who are you?

Through a public relations blitz that included playing patriotic songs around the clock on radio and television, using military planes to form hearts in the sky above Cairo and Alexandria, and circulating nationalist vemes on Facebook, the military entrenched the idea that being pro-military was equal to being pro-Egypt. El Sisi embodied the civilian and military options, the only viable solution.

From the other side, the Muslim Brotherhood had waited eighty years to capture the state. The group was not going to walk away from power so easily. The MB militias and their supporters took to the streets, carrying out attacks on citizens and police, and participating in the burning of over seventy churches and scores of other Christian-owned buildings. The MB e-militias rose again to spread a new pro-MB meme, a logo featuring a yellow-colored hand holding up four fingers to represent *Rabaa*, which means "four." The e-militias created scores of new pro-MB pages devoted to Rabaa al-Adaweya Square and its martyrs in order to spread the message that anyone who was anti-MB was a coup-supporter (*inqalabiyoon*), an anti-democrat, and a traitor to the revolution.

The two warring sides—the Islamists and the military—waged fierce battles for control over the minds and hearts of the

Figure 6.7: "Which do you prefer? El Sisi in his military uniform or in civilian clothes?"

Facebook youth. Facebook turned into a rumor mill, a platform for misinformation. Rumor vemes entered the space like virtual bombs exploding in the squares of social media. Facebook turned into a discredited space of lies and fake news. In this period of clashes between State Security and the Brotherhood, the "We Are All Khaled Said" page went mute. For the activists involved in the January 25 Revolution, and for the more democratically inclined revolutionaries, this moment became a time of reflection, silence, and confusion.

THE SQUARE OF CONFUSION

A new political terminology emerged to distinguish the January 25 Revolution of 2011, with its connection to Tahrir Square, from the revolution of June 30, 2013. Supporters of the Tamarud-led mobilization became known as belonging to the "First Square." The "Second Square" came to refer to supporters of the Muslim Brotherhood and their occupation of the Rabaa al-Adaweya Square. The "Third Square" was the name given to a group of activists who supported neither the military nor the Brotherhood, but a third way towards a civil democratic solution. On Facebook, social media citizens set up the page "The Fourth Square," the square that illustrates the contradictory positions and discourses of the politicians, which have led to a state of political confusion and doublespeak.

The cover photo of the Fourth Square page shows an imaginary square occupied by both military supporters and Morsi supporters. An Islamist stands in the center of the frame and says, "We are with democracy and against fans of democracy." In the square of confusion, the pro-MB symbol of the four fingers has El Sisi's name attached to it, and the El Sisi logo of the two hands in the shape of two Cs has the word "*Rabaa*" written underneath it.

The military and the Brotherhood, the two most powerful counter-democratic forces in society, were competing with each

Figure 6.8: The Fourth Square, the square of confusion and mixed messages

other to claim the title of revolutionaries. The actual revolutionaries went mute. They needed a period of reflection to understand how to break the military-Islamist cycle. They paused as they reevaluated ways to use their tools, platforms, networks, and creativity to bring about a more dramatic cognitive rupture with the past. How could they break the old mental frames and build new ones to spread the powerful memes that would pave the way for an alternative order?

CHAPTER SEVEN

The Anti-Ideology Machine

The January 25 Revolution, while in many respects a distinctly Egyptian and Arab event, also tells the global story of youth resistance in the digital age. Discontented youth around the world are searching for a new emancipatory paradigm. From the Arab uprisings that began with Tunisia in December 2010 and quickly spread to Egypt and other countries of the region, to the Occupy movement that popularized the slogan of the 99 percent, to the anti-austerity protest movements in southern Europe, to Taksim Square in Turkey, young citizens have been sending a clear and loud message: they reject the current economic and political system that neither respects nor nurtures them, and that denies them their dream of living with human dignity in a just and balanced global order. A central piece of the ongoing resistance movements has been concerned with the control of knowledge, the war of ideas, and struggles over who can pull the levers of ideology and culture to build an alternative order.

Rebellions and revolutions are never principally about overthrowing a tyrant or a sitting government and voting in a new one. They signify events when new actors insert themselves into the political arena to construct and spread a new narrative about the good society and how to achieve it. In the book *The Rebirth of History*, French philosopher Alain Badiou writes about the importance of the Idea, the new truth that must take root so that a rebirth of history can occur. This Idea cannot come from the dominant culture, for this is where the old ideas get reproduced. The new Idea must emerge from the margins, through a "popular initiative" outside the center of power. Badiou writes:

> Let us call these people, who are present in the world but absent from its meaning and decisions about its future, the *inexistent* of the world. We shall then say that a *change of world* is real when an inexistent of the world starts to exist in this same world with maximum intensity.[1]

The inexistent to which Alain Badiou refers are the excluded and disenfranchised groups—the poor, the workers, the geographically marginal, the minorities. Curiously, he does not refer to the young. If we look at Egypt and other countries around the world where uprisings and occupations of public spaces have taken place, the young are at the forefront. They suffer from all manner of political, economic, and social exclusion. They face escalating levels of insecurity about the future, whether measured in livelihoods or the condition of the planet. The global protest moment has allowed the inexistent to exist, to enter the public space and raise their voices. The problem is that their voices do not yet ring with a well-formed Idea about how to move forward.

Progressive philosophers and ordinary people alike are in agreement that we are searching for a new paradigm to build a more just, humane, and sustainable global order. The ideas and visions that will bring about global change are not yet part of the known human inventory of knowledge. Whence will the new ideas come? What can Egypt's social media wars elucidate about the battle for ideas in an age of uprisings that coincides with the age of the internet?

Whence Do the New Ideas Come?

Steven Johnson, the American media theorist and science writer, probes a timeless puzzle in his book *Where Good Ideas Come From: The Natural History of Innovation* (2010). Taking an environmental perspective, he argues that good ideas are not necessarily created during moments of epiphanies. Rather, ideas require an environment in which to gestate and evolve. For Johnson, good ideas are born when small non-completed ideas, or half-ideas, collide. In the Age of Enlightenment, the coffeehouse provided the environment for this process to occur. In the contemporary period, the internet offers the best chance for the circulation and birth of new ideas.

Johnson's theory, as insightful as it may be, suffers from the same deficiency as Richard Dawkins's meme theory. Neither author situates ideas within a political economy of knowledge. In other words, they do not acknowledge that not all great ideas have an equal chance of nourishment and survival. Those ideas that advance the current system of power—whether scientific, economic, or theoretical advancements—receive far more space and support to flourish through large commercial publishers, foundations, universities, and corporations, than ideas that challenge the current hierarchies of power. These dissenting ideas need to fight far harder for birth, survival, and propagation.

The ideas that will change history will not come about from a random collision of half-ideas in cyberspace. They will take shape from sharp and inquiring minds that are actively and consciously fighting the dominant culture and system of power. The medley of technologies and platforms, from social media and video games to mobile phones and satellite television, have all operated as tools, sites, and networks in the war of ideas and the battles over ideology. As the ongoing Egyptian uprising has shown, Egypt's tech-savvy virtual warriors have turned Facebook into an anti-system mechanism.

Young citizens have battled in virtual spaces and on the streets, sometimes to the death, to pose and answer questions as consequential as: Who can take part in conversations about how to imagine and realize a future society? What values will guide people as they struggle to build a new order? Who has the legitimacy to change and rule society? Which cultural artifacts and attitudes should be carried forward into the future, and which ones should be left behind as relics of the past?

The Egyptian case has also illuminated how communications technologies generally, and social media specifically, are tricky spaces to maneuver. They represent platforms in which existing powers and counter-powers vie for dominance in the war of ideas. The US State Department, the Muslim Brotherhood, and the Egyptian military have all had varying degrees of success uploading their ideology and convincing people that they alone are the true champions of democracy, the defenders of the revolution, and the protectors of the nation. The presence of the big powers and their proxies in virtual spaces has given rise to conspiracy theories and has led to much confusion about the Facebook factor in the Egyptian revolution.

Made-to-Order Uprisings?

In his 2012 book *Islam and the Arab Awakening*, Tariq Ramadan, the Swiss-Egyptian writer and grandson of Hassan al-Banna, uses the term "made to order uprisings" to refer to the 2010–2011 Arab revolts. Ramadan is but one in a chorus of voices supporting the idea that the January 25 Revolution was partially the result of a US-led conspiracy. According to Ramadan's analysis, Arab cyberactivists have been the proxies, the e-militias so to speak, of the US government:

> As early as 2004, but more systematically between 2006 and 2008, young people were trained by [American government-financed

nongovernmental organizations] … in the strategy and tactics of nonviolent mobilization: social networks and the use of symbols (the clenched fist appears … in Tunisia, Morocco, Egypt, and Syria). Not by any stretch of the imagination could the American, European, or even Russian governments have been unaware of these programs.[2]

He suggests, for reasons that remain unclear, that the US, with the aid of high-tech companies, pushed for regime change. He and other conspiracy theorists are especially wary of Google because of the company's close ties to the US government and military. Ramadan notes:

It is hard to ignore Google's position throughout the uprisings as being virtually identical to that of the US government or of NATO: explicit support for the Egyptian protesters, aimed at Mubarak's rapid departure; hesitations in Syria in the hope that domestic reforms would keep Bashar al-Assad's regime in power.[3]

In addition to Google's geopolitical entanglements, there is the fact that Wael Ghonim was a full-time employee at Google during his time as a coadmin of the "We Are All Khaled Said" page. Accusations and theories abound about Ghonim and whether he is an agent of the US. Many skeptics have pressed Ghonim to explain the nature of his relationship to Jared Cohen, the head of Google Ideas and formerly of the State Department. Ghonim remains cryptic on these questions. We cannot set the record straight about whether Ghonim was a willing agent, or if he was a naïve participant in something much larger than he was able to understand. While we do not deny the possibility of conspiracies, since we expect strong powers to use all means to achieve their interests, we are opposed to reducing multilayered events to misleading catchphrases like "made to order uprisings."

From the point of view of the conspiracy theorist, people are small, inconsequential victims of power, not the agents of history. Conspiracies also tend to obscure and mystify things that are in plain sight and that require only a critical and inquiring mind to see. The US has pursued, in full view and on the record, "pro-democracy" activist training as part of the Bush-era "War on Terror" and Obama-era "Internet Freedom" programs. A reading of US public diplomacy policies shows that they have had two principal goals: to contain Muslim youth so they do not become national security threats; and to attract youth from the MENA countries to a pro-US position by marketing American youth lifestyles and free-market values. In her historic policy speech on internet freedom on January 21, 2010, Secretary of State Hilary Clinton stated plainly the correlation between freedom and economic growth: "We feel strongly that principles like information freedom aren't just good policy, they're good business for all involved."

At this juncture, more important than asking whether Ghonim was an agent is to ask what revolutionary archetype he represents. Ghonim appears to be an Egyptian youth who believes in the entrepreneurial model of democracy, one in which marketing, profit, and freedom are interchangeable goals. This free-market approach to politics is precisely the model supported by the US State Department and the likes of Alliance of Youth Movement and CANVAS. These programs for cyberactivists were never intended to advance radical, revolutionary, or emancipatory politics, but to bring about a modicum of democratic reform while growing consumer markets in support of a US-led global political and economic order. It makes sense that the US establishment celebrated Ghonim as the face of the revolution while it entirely overlooked his coadmin, AbdelRahman Mansour, who is far more organically connected to Arab youth resistance movements and is recognized among young Arabs as a political thinker in his own right. *Time* magazine named Ghonim one of the hundred most influential people of 2011, and Caroline Kennedy presented him with a John F. Kennedy Profile in Courage Award. These honors were bestowed on Ghonim even though he had a scant political pedigree before the January 25 Revolution and essentially fled the political scene in the period following it.

In addition to the accolades, Ghonim received a seven-figure book deal with Houghton Mifflin Harcourt to write his memoir, *Revolution 2.0*. The slogan and subtitle of Ghonim's book, *The Power of the People Is Greater than the People in Power*, is bereft of emancipatory meaning. It is simply a marketing catchphrase. And being a professional marketer to the end, Ghonim hired the Harry Walker Agency to capitalize on his brand as Egypt's young revolutionary. The agency charged $35,000 for each of Ghonim's speaking engagements, not including ground transportation, hotels, and incidentals.

Irrespective of Ghonim's marketing approach to politics, the "We Are All Khaled Said" page was a phenomenon in the lead-up to January 25, 2011. It spearheaded one of the most dynamic youth movements in Egypt in perhaps half a century. The Khaled Said page attracted young Egyptians from across the ideological spectrum and provided a unique platform for interaction, deliberation, and creativity. The page worked to raise the consciousness of its members about civil disobedience and the Emergency Law. On the heels of the Tunisian uprising, one of the page admins, AbdelRahman Mansour, issued the call for the January 25 Revolution. Given its oppositional and mobilization credentials, can the "We Are All Khaled Said" Facebook page be considered part of the anti-ideology machinery? Was it a space that could give birth to the new Idea?

Egypt's Martyr Politics

The achievements of the KS page were truly remarkable, yet the page cannot be classified as an anti-ideology machine for two principal reasons: the KS movement relied on the historically and ideologically entrenched meme of martyrdom to achieve its ends, and it spread the meme of martyrdom through modern techniques of online marketing. Evoking martyrdom worked to rouse emotion, inspire action, and trigger revolt, but it did not give birth to a new Idea. Instead, the meme of martyrdom served to reinforce the logic of power and to ideologically constrain, rather than liberate, the community that rallied around Khaled Said.

At the hands of the two admins—a skilled marketer and young Arab activist of the digital age—Khaled Said became a blank slate on which to paint an aggregate portrait of an idealized everyday youth. In this airbrushed portrait, Khaled Said was transformed into a heroic champion of justice, a cyberactivist who was killed trying to fight the security forces. For the younger members of the page who were video game devotees, the fictitious script of Khaled very likely resembled an exciting video game story—a young hero who was killed fighting against the evil powers. The Khaled Said youth came together, determined to help Khaled posthumously get his retribution and fight the monsters who so brutally killed one of their own.

Figure 7.1: Video game mural on Mohamed Mahmoud Street, Cairo, July 2013. Photo by Mina Nabil

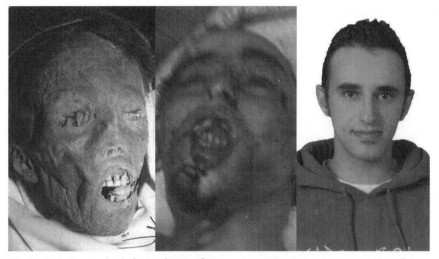

Figure 7.2: From the left: A photo of an ancient Coptic mummy, next to the iconic images of the martyr Khaled Said in death and life

Video game murals appeared at major battle sites in Cairo, testifying to the evocative power of the game. After a particularly deadly battle on Mohamed Mahmoud Street in Cairo, where young protesters fought to get retribution for the martyrs of January 25, revolutionary artists adorned the walls with massive murals depicting video game scenes that showed people prevailing against the evil police forces.

Video game dramas of good versus evil provided a reference point for some members of the Khaled Said community. Irrespective of virtual games, the martyrdom meme is buried deeply within the Egyptian psyche. To appreciate the historical embeddedness of martyrdom, we must take a more careful look at the morgue photo of Khaled. Just as Khaled's airbrushed portrait was familiar to Egyptians, so too was the graphic photo of Khaled's face in death, but in a different way. The image of Khaled's mutilated face resembles the faces of ancient Egyptian mummies who were canonized (Figure 7.2).

In ancient Egypt, the dead person worthy of mummification was transformed into a venerated saint and rewarded with eternal life. The royal mummies gained eternity as a birthright, whereas the saint-martyrs entered eternity by leading a life rife with extraordinary and heroic deeds. Saints left the world with tortured bodies—the cost of their virtue—but eternally pure hearts. Every saint requires a dramatic story full of innocence and heroism. Historically, the holy men and high priests crafted the martyrs' stories, but in today's society these stories are the domain of the blogger, the novelist, the marketer. When a person enters into sainthood, he or she assumes an aura of purity. From that point forward, no one should talk about the saint as a flawed human being, as someone with sin.

Like a mummy, Khaled Said was the innocent saint who was tortured to death at the hands of the corrupt and cruel oppressors. When Khaled Said crossed over into sainthood, he became cleansed of all imperfections. The real-life problems of the flesh-and-blood Khaled Said—an unemployed thirty-year-old youth who wanted to emigrate, who smoked and peddled hash, who hung out with people who neighbors described as delinquents—were forgotten and forbidden. These aspects of Khaled's life were not commensurate with the saint, whose role is to preserve Egypt's image as noble and honorable, not full of contradictions, flawed, and in need of deep introspection. Similar to the video game hero, the martyr-saint is the protagonist in a simple and moving story about a hero who fights the corrupt and unjust oppressor; and the oppressor is always "the other," never part of "the self."

Prior to the Khaled Said case, there were numerous other victims of police brutality and torture. The most famous torture victim was Emad El Kabir, whose brutal torture in a police station was filmed and uploaded to YouTube by an activist. Even through the video of El Kabir went viral, his story did not galvanize a wide base of supporters and get translated into a popular movement. There are two main reasons for this. To begin with, El Kabir survived the incident and therefore did not cross into the world of martyrdom. Second, and more significantly, his life as a petty drug dealer from a lower-class background appeared to be too unsavory for middle-class and moralistic Egyptians. The moral society quietly condemned the man for his uncouth lifestyle. Why could Egyptians rally behind the mythical middle-class saint-like figure of Khaled Said and not the real man Emad El Kabir? The answer can be found in the phrase "for the sake of Egypt's reputation" (*suma`t Misr*).

Fear of shame prevented the Khaled Said youth from moving outside of the frame of "the bad guys out there" versus "we the good guys in here." The group avoided introspection and coming to terms with the ways they themselves enacted real and symbolic violence on the "other" through attitudes and behaviors like sexism, religious discrimination, and denying the drug dealer his full humanity and due compassion.

This brings us back to the point about why asking whether Wael Ghonim was a foreign agent is the wrong question. More dangerous than the agent out there, that "other" who is working with foreign corporations and governments, is the agent within. We should pause to ask if we, the freedom fighters, the activists, the enlightened ones, the critical citizens, are in fact the real agents. Are we spreading the memes of power without even realizing it? To what degree have the system's memes—the ideologies that impede our humanity as they perpetuate behavior that accepts inequality, militarism, patriarchy, sexism, racism, and the destruction of life of all kinds—infiltrated our minds?

The stigma of shame led the Khaled Said youth to spread the message, "There are no drug dealers in Egypt, and there are no dealers among us. We are all The Saint." American philosopher Joan Copjec calls this mechanism of denial the "shame of the shame." She used this term in 2007 to describe why Iran's president Mahmoud Ahmadinejad (2005–13), when asked at a public lecture at Columbia University about the unfair treatment of homosexuals in Iran, replied that there were no gays in Iran. The ideological mechanism of "shame of the shame" works to keep unexamined, covered, and underground those behaviors, peoples, and views that do not correspond with the official mainstream version of the idyllic citizen in a mythically pure society.

In his magisterial work *Pedagogy of the Oppressed,* humanist philosopher-educator Paulo Freire speaks to the necessity of freeing the mind as a part of the struggle for human freedom. He entreats the person committed to freedom not to be afraid to face reality, to make the effort to doubt, to let go of certainty, "to see the world unveiled":

> The radical, committed to human liberation, does not become the prisoner of a "circle of certainty" within which reality is also imprisoned. On the contrary, the more radical the person is, the more fully he or she enters into reality so that, knowing it better, he or she can better transform it. This individual is not afraid to confront, to listen, to see the world unveiled.[4]

Looking back on the Khaled Said page, it was on the eve of the revolution, when members began debating sainthood and martyrdom and questioning their ethics and values, that the page had the potential to become an anti-ideology mechanism, a liberatory and radical space. This introspective moment was prompted by the story of Tunisia's martyr-saint, the self-immolator Mohamed Bouazizi. Young Egyptians questioned whether Bouazizi, a man who committed suicide, could be their symbol and inspiration. Their discussions raised ethical questions about icons, saints, religion, morals, and hierarchy, but these were cut short due to lack of time. The leaders needed to mobilize people quickly in order to be prepared for the revolt of January 25. They needed to hurriedly get ready for the "time of change," but with little thought to fundamental questions about change towards what, why, and for whom.

In the video series Big Think, Slovenian philosopher Slavoj Žižek delivers a message to activists about the value of thinking. He recognizes that people feel pressured to urgently do something in response to a deteriorating global economic, environmental, and political situation, yet he urges them to invest time in thinking prior to acting:

> Don't get caught in this pseudo-activist pressure. "Do something, let's do it," and so on. No! The time is to think … The famous Marxist formula was that philosophers have only interpreted the world, the time is to change it. Maybe in the twentieth century we tried to change the world too quickly. The time is to interpret it again, to start thinking.[5]

After the fall of Mubarak on February 11, 2011, the Khaled Said page lost its compass. It started to do things like lead calls for people to go out and clean the streets. A young activist commented, "We don't need the Khaled Said page to recruit us to clean the streets. We need it to lead us to clean our system from corruption, from all kinds of problems."

For all the ways the "We Are All Khaled Said" page provided a platform for youth awareness and broke barriers of political fear, it did not challenge the dominant ideology in a radical way. It opted for loyalty to the saint and its brand. A movement that relies on a mix of old historical memes and marketing can achieve many things, but it cannot give birth to the new Idea.

Virtual Intelligence

In a leaked video of a secret military meeting that took place in the months before the July 3, 2013, military takeover, General Abdel Fattah El Sisi explains the new rules of the media wars: "We are no longer in the era of censorship when we can prevent people from criticizing us. The time when no one can utter our name is over. At this time we need to work with secret hands." He goes on to talk about how, despite the fact that the revolution liberated society, the military is pursuing new ways to shackle the people and regain control over society. "The revolution has dismantled all the shackles that were present—not just for us, not just for the military, but for the entire state … The rules and the shackles were dismantled, and they are being rearranged."[6]

What precisely does El Sisi mean when he talks about "secret hands" and rearranging the shackles? He is talking about the need for the military, the pinnacle of hard power, to enter the arena of soft power in order to step up its game of ideological indoctrination. The old mechanisms of control based on instilling fear by means of force and censorship stopped working after the January 25 Revolution. Broad segments of the population, including children, youth, women, workers, professionals, Islamists, and the poor, shed their fear. General El Sisi understood that to pacify the population and make it governable again, the military needed to become more adept at using the machinery of ideology, combined with coercion.

In the three years since the start of the revolution, the Muslim Brotherhood has used the ideological machinery to spread a dogma of Islamism, whereas the military has spread a dogma of nationalism. At this stage only the most revolutionary, incisive, and liberated minds can fight these ideologies of control.

The ideas that can confront the dogmas are likely to come from the virtual spaces where an advanced kind of intelligence, what we call "virtual intelligence," is evolving. The revolutionaries who take social media seriously, these virtual warriors who effectively hone the disputative, creative, and subversive potentials of the space, possess a high degree of virtual intelligence. These warriors do not have a dogma; they reject dogma and are propelled forward by the goal of the anti-mechanism. They struggle to create anti-mechanisms by revealing, decoding, and derailing the ideological mechanisms of the system.

A beauty of virtual spaces is that anyone with access can excel as a virtual warrior. Virtual intelligence is not contingent on a person's formal schooling, material wealth, class position, religion, sex, age, or connection to power. In fact, people on the margins, whose minds are least controlled by the ideology of the system, are more likely to produce anti-system ideas. Being a successful virtual warrior requires the ability to innovate within the virtual architecture, to recognize the rapidly changing tenor of the cultural war, and to distinguish between pro-system and anti-system vemes.

Above all, the virtual warrior requires courage and determination. She understands that publicizing a post on Facebook, being an admin on a controversial Facebook page, making or circulating a controversial veme, comes with potential risks that range from being ostracized in the space to being arrested and even targeted for assassination. The warriors understand that there are consequences to their thinking and acting, but they push their ideas anyway because this is their society. They believe in their right to shape the community according to their values, their dreams.

The most radical virtual thinkers reject dogma and all that is holy and sacred, not out of nihilism but in an effort to free the mind. They create and think because they need something worthy that can respond to the moment, not because they are seeking a new permanent truth. In the war of ideas, nothing is sacred—not the symbol and blood of the martyr, nor even the revolution itself.

The radical Facebook page "Falota Fans" believes that now is the moment to kill all icons, even the icon of the revolutionary. The page posted the famous photo of Che Guevara taken shortly after his death. This last smile of the iconic revolutionary has inspired revolutionaries and artists all over the world. But instead of conveying an inspirational message, the words below the photo read, "This isn't an ordinary smile. This is the smile of a guy who sees cute virgins in heaven who are wearing the Soviet cap and dressed in red as they roll cigarettes for him" (Figure 7.3).

This unexpected and audacious caption not only criticizes Islamic notions about paradise, but also mocks the very notion

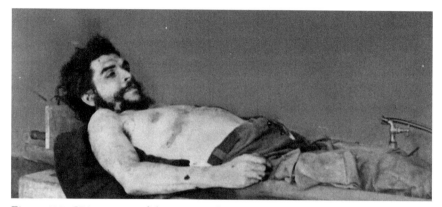

Figure 7.3: CIA picture of the executed Che Guevara

of the sacrifice and death of the revolutionary. It rejects the canon of dramatic narratives about the sacred blood and sacrifice of martyrs for the sake of the revolution, the sake of the nation. How can a warrior continue to be courageous, powerful, and effective without clear dreams, without dogma, without a utopian vision? Can a warrior go to the battle without ideology? Can the knight guide the horse to war without a banner? In such a moment, when the icons are shattered and the old taboos broken, a new story about the good society is possible. We can start from the zero level.

The new Idea cannot be invented in the womb of the dominant culture. This is the moment to doubt, question, and reevaluate our ethics and priorities. An anti-ideology machine should, by definition, set out to consciously change people's mental frames by sweeping away taboos, desacralizing icons, valuing life and dignity above the market, and freeing the mind. The revolutionaries described in this book are seeking to bring change through Facebook, the streets, the self. They are working to expose the mechanisms of dogma with their own anti-mechanisms. As in any war, they can win or lose. We cannot predict the future or know whether the Arab uprisings will lead to a new paradigm for global change, or whether they might move towards historical regression. All we can claim now is that the generations coming of age with social media, virtual values, and virtual intelligence have a great capacity to unlock the mechanisms of ideology. We must continue to struggle to keep these spaces free, to keep questioning, confronting, and creating on the way to a new truth, towards the rebirth of history.

Notes

1. WIRED YOUTH RISE

1. The three founders of the website were Hisham Morsey (a physician, a specialist in cancer cures, and a British/Egyptian dual national), Ahmed Adel Abdelhakeem (a chemist from Ain Shams University who went on to study political science in Vienna), and Wael Adel (a civil engineer from Ain Shams with a diploma in mass communications from Sudan).

2. CYBERDISSIDENT DIPLOMACY

1. D. Stojanovic and J. Gec, "Serbian Ousters of Milosevic Make Mark in Egypt," February 22, 2011. Retrieved from utsandiego.com.
2. P. Khanna, "Global Governance and Megadiplomacy," *The Brown Journal of World Affairs* 18.1, 2011, 25–34. Retrieved from bjwa.org.
3. According to USASpending.gov, Howcast received $524,500 from the State Department in 2008 and 2009 to support the development of digital services for cyberactivists. See Cuba Money Project, "U.S. Activist: 'Toppling Dictators is Something I Really Like,'" March 26, 2011, cubamoneyproject.org.
4. An Administration official said that Cohen "almost lost his job over it. If it had been up to the White House, they would have fired him." See R. Lizza, "The Consequentialist," *New Yorker*, May 2, 2011. Retrieved from newyorker.com.
5. K. Dozier, "CIA Open Source Center Follows Foreign Twitter, Facebook Accounts," *The Huffington Post*, November 4, 2011.

6. The chairman of the Adelson Institute is Natan Sharansky, former president of The Zionist Forum, former Interior Minister in Israel's Likud government, and a longtime pro-Israel and pro-Zionist advocate. The Adelson Institute deals with issues ranging from "democracy and security, to nationalism, terror and identity." See adelsonfoundation.org/AFF/newsroom.

3. MARKETING MARTYRDOM

1. The author would like to thank Amro Ali for conducting these interviews in the summer of 2011 as part of his investigative work on the life and death of Khaled Said.
2. An English Facebook page by the name "We Are All Khaled Said" was run by an independent admin not connected to the admins of the Arabic page. The two pages did, however, share some resources including videos about Khaled Said and news items about torture and the Emergency Law in Egypt.
3. All the posts referenced in this chapter and throughout the book originally appeared in Arabic and were translated by the authors.
4. W. Ghonim, *Revolution 2.0: The Power of the People Is Greater than the People in Power: A Memoir*, New York: Houghton Mifflin Harcourt, 2012, 59.

4. VIRTUAL VENDETTA

1. All direct quotes by AbdelRahman Mansour are taken from numerous interviews with him conducted by the author in 2011 and 2012 in Cairo.
2. These quotes about video games come from an unpublished interview conducted by Mark Lotfy with Bouka in 2012.
3. Ghonim, *Revolution 2.0*, 102.
4. A. Mansour, "The Upcoming Scenario of Change: The Egypt We Will Know in the Future," Al Jazeera Talk, May 10, 2008. (Original article in Arabic)

5. VIRAL REVOLUTION

1. Cited in R. Nasraoui, "Keynote Speech," Takaful 2012: Second Annual Conference on Arab Philanthropy and Civic Engagement: Selected Research, June 2012, Cairo: John D. Gerhart Center for Philanthropy and Civic Engagement. Retrieved from aucegypt.edu.
2. Y. Ryan, "How Tunisia's Revolution Began," Al Jazeera, January 26, 2011.
3. S. S. Al Qassemi, "Morsi's Win Is Al Jazeera's Loss," *AlMonitor*, July 1, 2012.
4. The Arabic Network for Human Rights Information, "The Internet in the Arab World: A New Space of Repression?" 2004.
5. Reporters Without Borders, "The 2005 World Summit on the Information Society in … Tunis: Someone's Got to Be Joking!" July 3, 2002. Retrieved from en.rsf.org.
6. J. Pollock, "Streetbook: How Egyptian and Tunisian Youth Hacked the Arab Spring," *MIT Technology Review*, August 23, 2011. Retrieved from technologyreview.com.
7. Reporters Without Borders, "The 2005 World Summit on the Information Society in … Tunis: Someone's Got to Be Joking!"
8. "Tunisia: Freedom in the World 2009," freedomhouse.org.
9. Pollock, "Streetbook: How Egyptian and Tunisian Youth Hacked the Arab Spring."
10. S. Garbaya, "The Other Dimension of the Virtual Space in the Revolution of Freedom in Tunisia: From Facebook to Streetbook." *North Africa Journal*, March 14, 2011.
11. C. Kang, " Tech Firms Hiring White House Staffers," *Washington Post*, March 28, 2011.

6. MEMES AND THE WAR OF IDEAS

1. R. Dawkins, *The Selfish Gene*, 2nd Edition, Oxford: Oxford University Press, 1990, 192.
2. For more details on the Rasd network see Rehab Sakr, "The Power of Online Networks: Citizenship among Muslim Brotherhood Cyber Youth," in L. Herrera, ed., *Wired Citizenship: Youth Learning and Activism in the Middle East*, New York: Routledge, 2014.
3. Ghonim, *Revolution 2.0*, 170.

4. G. Lakoff, *Whose Freedom?: The Battle over America's Most Important Ideas*, New York: Picador, 2006, 10.

7. THE ANTI-IDEOLOGY MACHINE

1. A. Badiou, *The Rebirth of History*, trans. by Gregory Elliott, London: Verso, 2012, 56.
2. T. Ramadan, *Islam and the Arab Awakening*, Oxford: Oxford University Press, 2012, 11.
3. Ibid., 12.
4. P. Freire, *Pedagogy of the Oppressed*, New York: Continuum, 1993, 21.
5. S. Žižek, "Slavoj Žižek: Don't Act. Just Think," YouTube, from the series Big Think.
6. The video was leaked by the RASSD news network (www.rassd.com) on October 5, 2013. Excerpts from the video, including the quote about the shackles, were quoted in D. Kirkpatrick, "In Leaked Video, Egyptian Army Officers Debate How to Sway News Media," *New York Times*, October 3, 2013.

Index

On the Typeface

This book is set in Minion, a typeface designed by Robert Slimbach for Adobe Systems in 1990, which has become one of the few contemporary book faces to rival the classic types of Caslon, Bembo, and Garamond. Though it has no obvious precursor, it retains a calligraphic sentiment that Robert Bringhurst dubs "neohumanist" in his *Elements of Typographic Style*.

Telltale features of Minion include the subtle cant in the bar of the "e," the angular bowl of the "a," and the tapered bulbs that terminate the head of the "a" and the tails of the "y" and "j."

Minion's restrained personality and even color have made it a popular workhorse type, the narrow set width of which provides economy yet does not detract from its suitability for book settings.